"For decades, James Sire has been an intellectual and cultural leader in the evangelical community. He has given voice to a wide range of topics important to the body of Christ. But his most recent book, *Apologetics Beyond Reason*, may well be his most unique offering. This is not anything like a standard apologetics book. While it contains reasons and arguments, it also brings together a wide range of 'pointers' to God that are often neglected. This well-researched book is sure to expand our understanding of apologetics. If it does, then many who previously were not interested in the subject will be drawn in to make their own unique contribution to the apologetic task."

J. P. Moreland, distinguished professor of philosophy, Talbot School of Theology, Biola University, and author of *The Soul: How We Know It's Real and Why It Matters*

"These are the learned and wry reflections of a man who has saturated himself in Christian truth, worldviews and apologetics for many years. It is rare for a reader to find such an author who has written so many thoughtful books (nearly all of which I have read) and engaged so many audiences with the glorious gospel of Jesus Christ. Please be one of those readers."

Douglas Groothuis, professor of philosophy, Denver Seminary, and author of *Christian Apologetics*

"James Sire's new work sparkles and delights. He does not merely offer us new arguments but new ways of seeing the world and ourselves. Not every reader will find every argument persuasive, but everyone will find something intriguing and thought provoking. This is a book on how the imagination can lead us to God that itself shows us the delights of the imagination."

C. Stephen Evans, professor of philosophy and the humanities, Baylor University

"This deeply thoughtful series of essays is an extraordinary apologetic beyond materialism. Sire addresses Christian humanists as well as the many secular humanists who are not materialists. Secular scholars and students in the humanities and many in the social sciences readily admit, as Christians do, that there is more to the world and human nature than the material of scientism. Sire, the master apologist who has given us so many great works, calls this book an 'eclectic apologetics.' Beginning with a dialogue between Descartes and Stanislaw Lem's robot Mymosh the Selfbegotten (as only Sire could do), the work is sprinkled liberally with literary giants and their characters across the ages, some Christian, some secular. He puts all these in dialogue with one another, with his own life, with our times and with Christianity. For the Christian humanities scholar and for all well-educated people, Christian or not, Sire has produced a masterpiece to engage, provoke and inspire."

Mary Poplin, professor of education, Claremont Graduate University, and author of *Is Reality Secular?* and *Finding Calcutta*

"James W. Sire has done it again. This is, literally, a masterful work. To borrow from him, Peter Kreeft and Ron Tacelli, 'There are the books of Jim Sire. Therefore God exists. You either see and hear this in his volumes or you don't.' I have seen and heard—thanks be to God. You must, too. Come, see and hear! And you might as well taste and smell and touch while you are at it."

David Naugle, professor of philosophy, Dallas Baptist University, and author of *Philosophy: A Student's Guide*

"Too often apologetics is seen as a battle of wits, with a hope that the best, most godly thoughts will vanquish all comers. Sire provides us with a genuinely personal apologetic, moving beyond the old-fashioned testimony and arguing from experience that our shared humanity is an amazing apologetic all its own: in our shared stories, in our shared experiences with beauty, in our shared nature with Christ and in our shared experiences of relating to the God who created us. A joyful conversation drawn from a life of amazing experiences that point to a God who loves us deeply."

Gene C. Fant Jr., provost, Palm Beach Atlantic University, author of *The Liberal Arts: A Student's Guide*

OTHER BOOKS BY JAMES W. SIRE

APOLOGETICS BEYOND REASON

WHY SEEING REALLY IS BELIEVING

> ◆ <

James W. Sire

IVP Academic

An imprint of InterVarsity Press
Downers Grove, Illinois

InterVarsity Press
P.O. Box 1400, Downers Grove, IL 60515-1426
World Wide Web: www.ivpress.com
Email: email@ivpress.com

InterVarsity Press® is the book-publishing division of InterVarsity Christian Fellowship/USA®, a movement of students and faculty active on campus at hundreds of universities, colleges and schools of nursing in the United States of America, and a member movement of the International Fellowship of Evangelical Students. For information about local and regional activities, write Public Relations Dept., InterVarsity Christian Fellowship/ USA, 6400 Schroeder Rd., P.O. Box 7895, Madison, WI 53707-7895, or visit the IVCF website at www.intervarsity .org.

Scripture quotations, unless otherwise noted, are from the New Revised Standard Version of the Bible, copyright 1989 by the Division of Christian Education of the National Council of the Churches of Christ in the USA. Used by permission. All rights reserved.

While all stories in this book are true, some names and identifying information in this book have been changed to protect the privacy of the individuals involved.

This book and Echoes of a Voice (Cascade, 2014) were completed at nearly the same time. These two books contain similar, sometimes identical, commentary on two of Hopkins's poems ("God's Grandeur" and "I wake and feel the fell of dark"), and Virginia Woolf's novel The Years. This and some further similar casual commentary is necessary to the arguments of both books. Wipf and Stock / Cascade Books (199 West 8th Avenue, Suite 3, Eugene, OR 97401) and InterVarsity Press have granted permission for this minor overlap between the books.

Cover design: Cindy Kiple
Interior design: Beth Hagenberg
Images: hole in black paper: © mattjeacock/iStockphoto
        blackboard equations: © alphaspirit/iStockphoto

ISBN 978-0-8308-4055-7 (print)
ISBN 978-0-8308-9649-3 (digital)

Printed in the United States of America ∞

Library of Congress Cataloging-in-Publication Data

Sire, James W.
  Apologetics beyond reason : why seeing really is believing / James W.
Sire.
      pages cm
  Includes bibliographical references and index.
  ISBN 978-0-8308-4055-7 (pbk. : alk. paper)
  1. Apologetics. 2. Christianity and the arts. I. Title.
BT1103.S567 2014
239—dc23
                                                                              2014012655

| P | 21 | 20 | 19 | 18 | 17 | 16 | 15 | 14 | 13 | 12 | 11 | 10 | 9 | 8 | 7 | 6 | 5 | 4 | 3 | 2 | 1 |
| Y | 32 | 31 | 30 | 29 | 28 | 27 | 26 | 25 | 24 | 23 | 22 | 21 | 20 | 19 | 18 | 17 | 16 | 15 | 14 |

To Marjorie

—faithful and patient, loving and kind—

♦

There is everything.

Therefore there is a God.

Either you see this or you don't.

Blessed are your eyes, for they see,

and your ears, for they hear.

Truly I tell you, many prophets and righteous people

longed to see what you see,

but did not see it,

and to hear what you hear,

but did not hear it.

—Jesus to his disciples (Matthew 13:16-17)

CONTENTS

PREFACE

>◆<

To see a world in a grain of sand,
And a heaven in a wild flower,
Hold infinity in the palm of your hand,
And eternity in an hour.

WILLIAM BLAKE, "AUGURIES OF INNOCENCE"

MY FRIENDS HAVE TOLD ME I HAVE A GOTHIC MIND; I'd call it Baroque. I see connections between some rather odd things and ideas. I am an inveterate and unrepentant punster. People groan their discontent as I interrupt a blossoming discourse with an off-topic pun. Only my daughter Ann can best me in verbal twisting. So while I will try not to indulge in displays of verbal talent in this book, I may find connections you will wonder about. Blake the poet wished to see the universe in a grain of sand. Me too.

My major thrust in this book is to come alongside you, point and say, "Look. Look carefully. Listen closely. Do you see? Do you hear?" There are a million signposts pointing toward the specific truth of God in Christ. I've seen many of them. But God is speaking to you too. Look and see. Listen and hear.

So this book is an eclectic apologetics. It mixes and matches various approaches to its subject. It contains a strange blending of autobiography and argument. It includes eccentric allusions to and arguments from the obscure (to most American readers) Stanislaw Lem to the obtuse (to too many readers) Gerard Manley Hopkins, and from the bare minimalism of Matsuo Bashō to the absurd chicanery of Lewis Carroll.

One important part of this eclectic argument is almost unique to apologetics literature. It has played a major part of my own developing understanding of both my Christian worldview and the reasons it is true. I will focus on the role of literature (and in broader terms, the arts) from a Christian point of view. But perhaps it's not unique. The following syllogisms also underlie the approach of Francis Schaeffer, though I strongly doubt that he would agree with the formulation.

The essence of the argument is this:

> There is literature.
> Therefore there is a God.
> Either you see this or you don't.

Or, more universal and primary:

> There is everything.
> Therefore there is a God.
> Either you see this or you don't.

Both, of course, are takeoffs on this syllogism from Peter Kreeft and Ron Tacelli:

> There is the music of Johann Sebastian Bach.
> Therefore there must be a God.
> You either see this or you don't.[1]

On the surface of it, all these syllogisms look absurd. They don't seem to embody reason at all. Surely they suggest a leap. No, not a leap of faith, but a leap beyond reason to sudden, intuitive direct perception of reality. Seeing really is believing. So is hearing.

ACKNOWLEDGMENTS

> ◆ <

MUCH OF THIS BOOK IS AUTOBIOGRAPHICAL, and there is no end to those who have played a part in it—that is, in the development of my understanding of Christian life, theology and apologetics; philosophy; and literature and literary criticism. In fact, everyone in any of these fields whom I quote or cite has been influential in one way or another. Of course, too, my family—from even before my grandfather Paul Louis Eugene Sire came to the United States from Switzerland—has played a role, for both fact and myth are involved. But it's high school teachers like Lavonne Johnson and college professors like Lewis McNew at Washington State, Donald Clark and Ed Costello at the University of Missouri, and Arthur Holmes at Wheaton College (Illinois) whose names are not cited in this book who have been chief among my academic mentors.

As for family, it is, of course, my wife who deserves the most recognition. I suspect that lots of male writers acknowledge their wives for their own safety's sake. When I say that without her help my manuscripts would never have gotten past the first readers in ten dozen publishing houses, I am not exaggerating. Well, not much. She was a typesetter for many years. Her proofreading eyes and sense of rhetorical propriety are stellar. She will have read this before it goes off to press. Thanks, Marj!

Publisher Jim Nyquist and editors Steve Board and Jim Hoover have seen to it that my work has gotten published in years past. And now editors Andrew Le Peau and especially Brannon Ellis have been the shepherds. It's a delight for me that Ruth Goring had her hand in this book at the very end; she's my favorite copyeditor. What a great crew there has been at InterVarsity Press since I joined them in 1968!

It is embarrassing, terribly dishonoring, to mention all these men and women and not first to have thanked God. But I don't quite know how to thank him in public. So I will just say, praise God in whom we live and move and have our being!

1

THE PAST AS PROLOGUE

God Adumbrations in Many Daily Forms

>◆<

Consolers cannot always be truthful. But very often, and almost daily, I have strong impressions of eternity. This may be due to my strange experiences, or to old age. I will say that to me this does not feel elderly. Nor would I mind if there were nothing after death. If it is only to be as it was before birth, why should one care? There one would receive no further information. One's ape restiveness would stop. I would miss mainly my God adumbrations in the many daily forms.

MR. ARTUR SAMMLER TO DR. GOVINDA LAL IN SAUL BELLOW'S
MISTER SAMMLER'S PLANET

"GOD ADUMBRATIONS IN THE MANY DAILY FORMS"[1]: this could be the subtitle to this book. It's what Mr. Sammler wants. Mr. Sammler, an elderly Jewish refugee from World War II in Poland, walks and thinks his way through the streets of New York. He has not given up on immortality. But he's willing to live with what he most wants to keep—his "God adumbrations in the many daily forms."

I am not so willing to give up immortality. I rest myself in the hope of glory, "Christ in you," as the apostle Paul said. Indeed, the presence of Christ signaled those God adumbrations Mr. Sammler so enjoyed.

Mr. Sammler was old. So am I. Mr. Sammler's life was messy—much messier than mine. But mine has been messy enough. In fact, no human life, even in retrospect or *sub species aeternitatis,* ever looks straight and narrow. And because of that, neither does any effective apologetic for the Christian faith.

AN INITIAL DEFINITION OF APOLOGETICS

I will begin my story and the story of this book with the slightly revised, broad definition of apologetics that opened my *Little Primer on Humble Apologetics*:

> Christian apologetics lays before the watching world such a winsome embodiment of the Christian faith that for any and all who are willing to observe there will be an intellectually and emotionally credible witness to its fundamental truth.[2]

This notion of apologetics serves for both seekers and believers. Then I added this:

> The success of any given apologetic argument is not whether it wins converts or strengthens the faith of any given believer, but whether it is faithful to Jesus. The reasons that are given, the rhetoric that expresses these and the life of the apologist and the larger community of faith must, then, demonstrate their truth.

This definition is broad based. It says nothing about which reasons count and which sorts of rhetoric are useful. In this book, I want to say something about both. You will not find here either an exhaustive catalog of proper reasons and reasoning or a demonstration of proper rhetorical principles. Rather, I have focused on a small, eclectic collection of both.

THE COMPLEX MAP OF APOLOGETICS

One background for this book is the history of apologetics and its range from complex argument to direct perception, from elaborate scholarly tomes to brief conversations with friends, from the rhetorical forms of autobiography, novel, poetry, drama and essay to blogs, radio spots and YouTube clips. I'm an old guy, but I still remember a brief radio drama from the National Council of Churches, broadcast sometime in the 1950s or 60s. I present it from memory in the sidebar.

POPULAR APOLOGETICS

A visitor from a nearby church knocks on the door of a house of a neighbor. "Good afternoon, sir," he says to the man who answers the door. "I'm John Buck from the big church down the street, First Church of the Resurrection. I'd like to invite you to join us in worship next Sunday. It's at 9:30 and we'd love to have you."

"Hmm. Next Sunday, you say? Well, I'll be golfing then."

"No problem. We meet every Sunday to sing and get to know each other. It's interesting and sometimes even fun, especially when you stay after the service for coffee and donuts. How 'bout the next Sunday? I'd be glad to walk down with you and your family and introduce you to some pretty nice people."

"Oh, that won't work either. Our family is leaving for vacation on the Friday before that."

"Oh, sure, I understand. How 'bout when you get back?"

"Well, I'll be pretty tied up getting our new ad campaign going at work. That'll involve several weekends."

"And after that?"

"Gosh, I could be dead by that time."

"That's right."

This ad, of course, focuses on getting a hearing for the gospel, but, simple as it is, it contains an implicit apologetic.

Judeo-Christian apologetics is as old as Job and as new as the latest clever tweet or YouTube clip. For the purposes of this book most of the history in between can be left to others. But one section—the past seventy years or so—is highly relevant to what I am trying to accomplish now.

I grew up in an age when most thoughtful people placed confidence in reason, not just in commonsense everyday reasoning but in reason as a path to sure knowledge, both the abstract knowledge of philosophy and theology and the earthbound knowledge of science. I read the major Christian apologists then popular with thinking Christians. They included philosophically oriented theologians like Carl F. H. Henry, Edward John Carnell and Bernard

Ramm; philosophers like Gordon Clark, Gordon Lewis and Arthur Holmes; and literary scholars and writers like C. S. Lewis and G. K. Chesterton.

Along the way I also read the work of those they inspired—Norman Geisler, Alvin Plantinga, Nicholas Wolterstorff, William Lane Craig, J. P. Moreland, Ronald Nash, and later Alister McGrath, Lee Strobel and Tim Keller. As editor for InterVarsity Press, I oversaw the publications of rationally grounded apologists like Douglas Groothuis, Clark Pinnock and several clever followers of Lewis and Chesterton (like Peter Kreeft and Paul Chamberlain). Except for Lewis and Chesterton and, to a lesser extent, the work of their followers, the evangelical apologists of the 1960s and after usually took on the limitations imposed by the modern acceptance of the autonomy of human reason. While they well knew that the human ability to reason requires a firmer foundation than the naturalism that was inherent in this assumption, they wanted to start on a common ground. The ground they chose was the trust that modernity placed in the ability of reason to reach true conclusions.

Their rationalist reasoning took several forms. Some of their arguments began with principles that many people took as self-evident, added other truths (principles and empirical evidence), and argued with sophistication for the existence of God, the deity of Jesus, the historical reliability of the narrative accounts in Scripture and the resurrection of Jesus. They addressed intellectual objections to their arguments and answered tough questions arising from the traditional Christian faith (the problem of evil, epistemological relativism, alternative claims of other religions, the challenges of science, etc.). Sometimes they turned challenges on their head, arguing, for instance, that the results of modern sciences such as the physics of astronomy make the notion of a personal Creator more likely than any alternative explanation.

For those in our culture who put their trust in human reason, these apologetic approaches have worked well. Many Christians today read and benefit from them. Without them, thoughtful Christians would have too few resources to analyze the clever arguments and glossy lifestyles presented by our culture's media, its pundits, its fraudulent experts and its passionate prophets of health and wealth.

But many in our postmodern world have come willy-nilly to distrust reason, and the arguments of the modern Christian rationalists now seem irrelevant, doubtful, lifeless. The approaches of C. S. Lewis and G. K. Chesterton avoided this fate by clever and imaginative grasps of the paradoxes of the human condition. The value of human reason for them was to permit a conclusion to be wrested from within a framework of paradoxes. It took account of the human desire for simplicity, tied the reader in knots and then showed how Christian faith both accounted for the knots and then untangled them. Their work has attracted readers from across the intellectual spectrum from the simple to the sophisticated.

But highly sophisticated rational apologetics itself is limited to those who can understand it. I, for example, don't understand why the *kalam* cosmological argument succeeds.[3] I suspect that there are legions of intelligent people like me. I've pondered the argument, I think I understand it, but I keep seeing objections I don't think have been answered. Of course, the problem could well be my own inability to grasp the argument, rather than a weakness of the argument itself. In any case, the *kalam* argument doesn't work for me.

There is another limitation in many arguments Christians use to prove the rationality of belief in God. The God who is "proved" is only a transcendent, impersonal God, maybe a Creator, but not necessarily personal. Only a God whose existence is important to human understanding or human flourishing is worth troubling about. The arguments may support deism as a worldview but be silent about the existence of a fully biblical God. Of course, such arguments can be stepping stones to a fuller argument for the God of the Bible. And that's no small matter.

Actually, some of my own arguments of a less sophisticated type lead first to the existence of a vague transcendence on which further arguments can build. So take my criticism of the *kalam* argument with a grain of salt. We must grant value to arguments for the existence of the transcendent God, even if not the fully biblical God.

There are many sophisticated arguments that I do understand, not by any means completely, but well enough to be satisfied that they support a Christian worldview. I am not complaining about rational apologetics as such but about what often seems to be assumed by many who use it—to wit, that *it is a highly effective approach and should work even if it doesn't.*[4]

In the late 1960s and 70s a new sort of apologetics arose from the lectures and publications of Francis Schaeffer. Instead of arguing from so-called self-evident principles, he began by recognizing the role of culture, especially painting and literature. He identified the presuppositions—the unstated foundation of cultural artifacts, values and ideas—that were either assumed or promoted by literature and painting. Then he showed how those ideas failed to account for the rich fabric of human being and human life, what in the 1970s he could still call "the mannishness of man." Working from the Bible down and from the culture up, he understood the mindset of the counterculture and showed the profound relevance of Western culture to our understanding of God. Schaeffer wanted to show that the God who is really there is not any of the gods of the day—the mystical constructs of emotion and desire.

On the one hand Schaeffer, like Carl Henry, relied on the ability of the human mind to reason rationally. He justified this by explaining the biblical foundation for human reason: human beings are made in the image of God and, even in their fallen state, retain the ability to reason—not from the inside out but from the outside in—from Scripture and God's revelation in nature. He insisted that there was such a thing as "true truth" but moderated that with the notion that one can know some but not all of such truth. His was a chastened rational apologetic, a version of presuppositionalism that spanned the gap between modern rationalism and the birth and then the burgeoning of postmodernism.

Working to and from the existentialists, C. Stephen Evans in his first book crafted an approach paralleling Schaeffer's.[5] And Os Guinness expanded Schaeffer's approach with his recognition of the value of thinking in the categories of sociology as well as philosophy.[6] Today, moreover, there are apologists who take a humble stance concerning the value of rational argument. Some of this movement can be seen, I hope, in the books I have written.

A CONFESSION GOOD FOR MY SOUL

Now let me turn to my own place in the story of recent apologetics—a miniautobiography via bibliography.[7] I offer it as a retrospective—where my mind, for good or ill, has been. It partly explains why I am finally willing to say that everything points to God. The view may be eclectic and eccentric. You judge. You use your reason, the good sense God has given all of us. Ah, but do it kindly, please.

My early books were largely grounded in modern rationalism, but as I lectured and wrote, I came to see two things—the growing failure of arguments to move students and others toward Christian faith and the rising possibility of doing apologetics with attention to why people today actually do become Christians.

My first book to strike a chord with readers was *The Universe Next Door: A Worldview Catalog* (1976). It came from twelve years of teaching world literature from Homer to Camus and English literature from Beowulf to Virginia Woolf. I learned the notion of worldview from Donald Clark at the University of Missouri, where I studied and taught from 1958 to 1964. The book that emerged combined a history of worldviews with a host of illustrations from the great literature of the world. I used the definition and comparison of worldviews to show the superior ability of Christianity to explain our experience and thus offered an apologetic for the Christian worldview.

How to Read Slowly (1978) explained how to read literature "worldview-ishly," that is, how to detect and evaluate the views of reality explained by or adhered to by authors. This book was not an apologetic in itself, but it was a step toward understanding the apologetic character of literature. And *Scripture Twisting* (1980), deriving from my frustration with wild and often foolish misreadings of the Bible by those promoting a heretical Christianity or alternative religion, belongs to a subspecies of more scholarly works focused on the correct reading of Scripture.

Meanwhile, *The Universe Next Door* was well received by a wide group of readers—students, teachers and apologists. Even some teachers who were not Christian used the book for its labeling and descriptions alone. From this success came many invitations to speak to university and college students and faculty in North America, and eventually in Eastern Europe after the Berlin Wall came down.[8]

As a speaker I was largely an apologist. A book form of several of my arguments emerged in *Chris Chrisman Goes to College: And Faces the Challenges of Relativism, Individualism and Pluralism* (1993). The book follows the first-year college experience of Chris, my version of a naive (aren't all "freshmen" naive?) evangelical Christian. It reflects my growing awareness that the categories of sociological analysis can illuminate for apologists a fuller picture of the culture(s) we address than those of mere intellectual analysis.

One of my lectures given first in the 1980s under the title "Why Should Anyone Believe Anything at All?" became a standard of my speaking fare. Some years later it morphed into *Why Should Anyone Believe Anything at All?* (1994), an expanded version of the talk. That book is still my best shot at an apologetic covering the major issues faced by people today. Its method is a bridge between modernist and postmodernist apologetics. Given as a talk, it assumes that those listening have not thought much about why they believe whatever it is they believe. In the course of a dialogue with the audience, I try to demonstrate that they actually do not act as if different beliefs, different religious conceptions, are equally true. They actually act as if they believe because their own belief is *true*—true in the sense that the opposite of that belief cannot be true. Many of the audience came to see this. In any case, the sponsors must have thought so, because this became the talk I was most invited to give.

My approach was to return students from a postmodern model of reality to a model of reality that takes truth seriously. Eventually, I wanted people to see that the Christian worldview better explains the character and value of rational thinking (as in science) than what they had absorbed by osmosis from their experience in the classrooms of the nonscience disciplines and in their life in the dorms.[9]

Two books followed. *Habits of the Mind: Intellectual Life as a Christian Calling* (2000) again stressed the importance of clear thinking that is also humble and deeply emotional. *Václav Havel: Intellectual Conscience of International Politics* (2001) exemplified the practical value of worldview analysis in understanding and assessing the contributions of key cultural figures as expressed in their philosophical and literary works. This book became a distinct apologetic when it concluded that the stunning ethical insights and practices of this great thinker, dramatist, political dissident and activist could be better undergirded by a Christian conception of God than by his notion of the Horizon of Being.

By the turn of the century, worldview analysis had become both widely used by thoughtful Christians and widely criticized for being overly intellectual. When David Naugle wrote his massive history of the worldview concept, he argued that worldviews are rooted in personal commitment, a matter of the heart, more than being a mere matter of the intellect. In

Naming the Elephant (2004) I focused on this profound insight, and I revised my early definition of worldview to reflect it.

After this I returned to write two tightly focused works of apologetics. *Why Good Arguments Often Fail* (2006) could be subtitled "the confessions of a failed apologist." It was a call to combine excellent reasoning with excellent rhetoric. *A Little Primer on Humble Apologetics* (2006) outlined what I take to be my mature understanding of apologetics.[10] It contains the definition of apologetics that I quote above. In short, I see apologetics not so much as argument as a call from Christians to all others to look, to see, to grasp by whatever means at their disposal the truth of the Christian faith and follow up by a commitment to Jesus Christ as Lord and Savior.[11]

Deepest Differences: A Christian-Atheist Dialogue (2009), coauthored with Carl Peraino, an atheist and retired cancer researcher, is a perfect illustration of two series of rational arguments that failed—my own and my opponent's. We each then explain from our own point of view why we had failed to change the other's mind. The result does not bode well for reason's effectiveness. More recently my memoir *Rim of the Sandhills: Why I Am Still a Christian* (2012) has been published as an ebook (Kindle and Nook).

As the present book is published, so is my *Echoes of a Voice* (Cascade, 2014). The two books are similar and different. The present book focuses on the wide variety of good arguments and evidence for Christian faith in literature and elsewhere. *Echoes of a Voice,* a larger tome, singles out *signals of transcendence,* delving deeply into their nature and to the varying ways they have been interpreted within the frameworks of different worldviews.[12]

APOLOGETICS IS MESSY

As the brief history of apologetics suggests and the flow of my own changing mind shows, apologetics is messy. Our multicultural world has formed us in diverse ways. We are eclectic—each of us a bit of this, a bit of that—but still one unique person. We live together with deep differences. Our lives are not under the control of the intellect alone. Feeling and desiring fuel who we are, what we value and how we behave. We are a messy people, a fallen people, and that messy fallenness poses a challenge to those who engage in apologetics.

Still we can ask: among all the ways apologetics can be done, is there a best way? The answer is clearly no. Here are four simple reasons. First, what can be known about God, his character and his intentions for us is massive, beyond our capacity to grasp. Second, the content of the Christian faith is so rich, so complex, so variegated, so deep, that it too is beyond human grasp. Third, human beings, the recipients of this knowledge, are so complex, so variegated, so profound that no single approach will succeed in addressing them. Finally, all of us—apologist and apologee—are fallen. Add fallenness to finitude, and we can see that effective apologetics can result only when the Holy Spirit becomes active in both the sender and the receiver of the message.

Every approach possible short of trickery, terror and subliminal coercion can be the best. The context—culture, ethnicity, education, gender, age, situation—will serve to make the task messy. Still, the goals will remain the same: to lay "before the watching world such a winsome embodiment of the Christian faith that for any and all who are willing to observe there will be an intellectually and emotionally credible witness to its fundamental truth."

Success in any argument is never under the control of the arguer, and it should not be. In the final analysis, God inspires the work of the apologist and then uses it as he wills.[13]

So messiness in apologetics is a given. The book that follows is an illustration. It emphasizes neither deductive arguments from principles nor inductive arguments from data. Both sorts of rationality appear in the following account, but they do not characterize the overall approach. The message is a story; the messenger is wrapped up in pilgrimage; that, too, is a story. My own movement from a first encounter with striking *signals of transcendence* through a typical evangelical experience of salvation and on to the development of a richer understanding of the faith and the reasons that both keep that faith from being blind and demonstrate the depth of a faith that is intellectual, emotional and practical—all of that is story. So too, you and every other reader of this book are in a story that is encompassed by the story of creation, fall, redemption and glorification. And either you'll see this or you won't. To see this is to believe it.

2

WONDERING ABOUT GOD

An Argument from René Descartes and Stanislaw Lem

I do not now admit anything which is not necessarily true:
to speak accurately, I am not more than a thing which thinks,
that is to say a mind or a soul, or an understanding, or a reason,
which are terms whose significance was formerly unknown to me.
I am, however, a real thing and really exist; what thing?
I have answered: a thing which thinks.

RENÉ DESCARTES, "MEDITATION II"

THIS CHAPTER JUMPS BACK AND FORTH, interweaving my story and my argument. Hang on for the ride. And hang with me.

Over the many years from the seventh grade till today, my commitment to Christ has not radically changed. My basic beliefs have remained traditionally Christian. What has changed are the reasons I give for believing the Christian faith to be the true explanation of the way *things are what they are*. So how are things? I will begin with what some might think is an audacious claim. It's nothing new. It fits solidly within a Christian worldview. But recently I have begun to have a greater sense of its truth and the power of its implication for my life and for my approach to apologetics. The claim is this:

There is nothing in the universe that does not finally point to the existence of God as Father, Son and Holy Spirit.

From the tender love a mother shows for her child to the anger of the villain who would dash a child's head against a rock, from the vastness of the universe to the minute and invisible wave-particles of light, from the history of the human race to the existence of one person in one place and one time—everything points to the triune God.

Blaise Pascal put it this way: "What can be seen on earth indicates neither a total absence, nor the manifest presence of divinity, but the presence of a hidden God. Everything bears this stamp."[1] Everything shows that there is a transcendence that surely exists but is hidden. Well, as Pascal would say, that is often hidden but sometimes blazes like fire.[2]

But wait. Surely an argument that maintains that there is no effective argument against it is a proclamation, not an argument. Let this objection stand. Over this and the next few chapters, I will try to explain why the argument is neither audacious nor merely a proclamation. I will pay special attention to literature but will also glance at many of the sorts of things that everything ultimately is.

For the moment, I simply wish to come alongside you as a reader, point and say, "Look. Look carefully. Listen closely. Do you see? Do you hear?" There are a million signposts toward the specific truth of God in Christ. The few I mention will, I trust, become some of them for you.

But where can I begin this journey through the messiness of both my mind and modern apologetics? The beginning, of course. The Bible begins this way: "In the beginning God . . ." Is that a clue, a signal? Let's find out. How shall we think about God?

A LIFE OF THE MIND

The title of this chapter may be deceiving. I am not going to take one of Descartes's three arguments for the existence of God and agree with it or make it my own. Quite the contrary: I will argue that the very failure of Descartes's arguments makes a case for the existence of God. But let's go slow here. Let me continue with my story, especially with my fascination with philosophy itself.

"Philosophy begins in wonder," Aristotle said. That was certainly true of my interest in philosophy, my practice of which began early, though the

THE GLORY OF GOD IN THE FACE OF CHRIST

When our hearts turn to him, that is opening the door to him, that is holding up our mirror to him; then he comes in, not by our thought only, *not in our idea only, but he comes himself, and of his own will.* Thus the Lord, the Spirit, becomes the soul of our souls, becomes spiritually what he always was creatively; and as our spirit informs, gives shape to our bodies, in like manner his soul informs, gives shape to our souls.

In this there is nothing unnatural, nothing at conflict with our being. It is but that the deeper soul that willed and wills our souls, rises up, the infinite Life, into the Self we call *I* and *me,* makes *I* and *me* more and more his, and himself more and more ours; until at length the glory of our existence flashes upon us, we face full to the sun that enlightens what is sent forth, and know ourselves alive with an infinite life, even the life of the Father. Then indeed we *are*; then indeed we have life; the life of Jesus has, through light, become life in us; the glory of God in the face of Jesus, mirrored in our hearts, has made us alive; we are one with God forever and ever.

—George MacDonald, *Creation in Christ* (Wheaton, IL: Harold Shaw, 1976), quoted by Rueben P. Job and Norman Shawchuck, *A Guide to Prayer for Ministers and Other Servants* (Nashville: Upper Room, 1983), p. 267

formal study began rather late. I don't mean to claim that I was a philosopher before I studied philosophy. Nor, even though I have taught philosophy, do I mean that I became one later. It was simply that intellectual curiosity—for good or ill, rewarded with truth or bound by self-deception—came early. I wouldn't have called my curiosity philosophy, but it was philosophic. I wondered about God and the universe, I asked questions and I pondered.

My first conscious bout with philosophy came as a question in theology. "If God is all powerful and he wanted everyone to be Christian, why didn't he make them so they would choose to follow Christ? Why would he allow so many to reject him or make it so difficult for some even to know about him?" I was in the seventh or eighth grade, and my friend Don Dix and I had puzzled over this issue. So we asked his father, expecting to get a good, clear answer.

His father, Earl, was a missionary to the then Belgian Congo on furlough back in his and my hometown of Butte, Nebraska. Surely he would know. I do not remember the answer he gave. But for some years I continued to wrestle with predestination, free will and the final fate of those who never hear the gospel. I've read Luther and Erasmus and many modern theologians and philosophers. But while I have come to terms with the question itself, I still do not have an answer that is set in concrete. Nor is any answer, like the bodies of some dead Mafia members, buried in concrete. For me there has been no Lutheran "Here I stand; God help me" moment regarding the issue of predestination and free will.

My first philosophy course came midway in my academic career. I had graduated from the Arts and Sciences College of University of Nebraska with "minimum" majors in both chemistry and English. That degree prepared me for nothing—well, nothing lucrative. So the summer of 1955 I worked in an agricultural chemistry lab and took three courses—two to partially prepare me to teach in high school and one for fun, Introduction to Philosophy. That course was monumental in shifting my attention more and more from science to the liberal arts. The professor assigned Plato's *Dialogues* and Bertrand Russell's *Problems in Philosophy*. These choices were perfect for me. Both philosophers are superb writers. As a student and avid reader of literature, I loved that. Both further piqued my interest in matters esoteric. I was spellbound and hooked.

When my brief military career began in September of that year, I stuffed a paperback edition of Bernard Berenson's *Aesthetics and History* inside my khaki shirt and read it during the boring military classes at Aberdeen Proving Ground, Maryland. Why I never got caught I'll never know. Six months later I began buying most of the few books on philosophy in English that I found in a small bookstore in Seoul, Korea, where I served as a shavetail lieutenant. I also enrolled in a logic course from the University of Maryland taught by extension, a course I started but never finished. Oops! Was that a hint of what was to follow?

Seeking an MA in English at Washington State College, I took two courses in junior college education. These were interesting and valuable, but they did not do for me what two courses in philosophy would surely have done. On the way to the PhD in English at the University of Missouri, however, I finally made a wise decision. For the required twelve hours in a field related to English, I chose philosophy. My courses concentrated on Plato, Plotinus (the most significant Neoplatonist who influenced Christian theology of the Middle Ages and English literature of the Renaissance), philosophic ideas in literature and Continental rationalism (Descartes, Leibniz and Spinoza). In these courses I was finally in my element.

Graduate students in English who take a minor in philosophy may be doing so as pretentious dabblers. Or so one of my English professors thought. So he asked the chairman of the philosophy department, who was also my teacher in Continental rationalism, "Is Jim Sire a dilettante?" My English professor later told me that he was assured that I was not. That, I thought, was a close call.

A Child of Descartes

One thing is clear to me. I have been a child of Descartes. I have wanted answers to my curiosity that were both true and philosophically certain. I wanted what Descartes believed he achieved when, after mulling over what he could and could not doubt, he concluded that one thing was absolutely certain: "I think, therefore I am." This was so certain, said Descartes, that it could not under any circumstance be false. Anyone, he thought, would have to conclude that he was right. "I think, therefore I am" became for Descartes the foundation for his whole philosophical system.[3]

I wanted what Descartes wanted—certainty with regard to the existence of God and the truth of the Christian faith. During my early years in graduate school at the University of Missouri, I struggled in this quest. I never dangled on a thin rope of belief over a precipice of haunting doubt. I always believed that my faith in Christ was well placed. But I thought that among all the intelligent people who still believed in the truth of Christianity, there must be someone, probably lots of someones, who could put an end to my search for certainty.

I found that someone in theologian Bernard Ramm, though his answer was not cast in the form of a rational argument.[4] Rather it was a justification for belief on the basis of the internal witness of the Holy Spirit. I remember the great relief that came when I realized that there would be no rational argument that would prove forever and ever beyond a shadow of a doubt that any part of my faith was true. I have since come to the conclusion that no belief, no knowledge, can have that kind of certainty. Twenty years later Lesslie Newbigin, from a somewhat different perspective, provided further justification for my rejection of an Enlightenment approach to certainty.[5] A reason for certainty of another origin and type would come, as I will explain later.

Over the years friends have accused me of being a rationalist and its opposite, a fideist, or even a mystic. I am none of these. For most of my life as a Christian and an apologist, I have been a presuppositionalist.[6] That is, I believed that all our arguments are finally based on assumptions—notions to which we are fundamentally committed. In short, they are pretheoretical. But our conscious or even unconscious commitment to them need not be blind. And when we discover we have made these commitments, we need not be constantly in doubt, as if it were the power of our will to believe that gives us confidence that our commitments are well placed. In fact, if we work at it, we can discover what our pretheoretical commitments are, and we can determine whether they are likely to be sound. One way is to argue to a *best explanation.*[7] Another way is to consciously recognize how we, being made in the image of God, participate in the reality of God himself. This second way may sound bizarre. I will explain it in chapter three. But first I will explain *best explanation,* otherwise known as *abductive reasoning.*

We all believe that we exist, do we not? Who, then, are we? How do we know that our answer to that question is accurate?

What are the alternatives? Here are a few:

1. Our self-consciousness and ability to think are undesigned; they evolved from nonrational physical material by chance and necessity.

2. In the process of physical evolution an intelligent alien race invaded our bodies.

3. They didn't invade our bodies but they tweaked our DNA so that we developed minds that appear to work quite well.

4. We were somehow intentionally made by an omniscient God in his image.

None of these is so certain that it cannot be doubted. Moreover, there may be others that give a better explanation. But at least 1 and 4 have more plausibility than 2 or 3. The literature of biology, philosophy and theology is vast. There is God's plenty to stoke the furnace of our minds. We needn't make our decision by casting lots or choosing blindly.

Option 4 is basically the view taken by Christians. The justification for it would take us into a huge realm of data and reasoning. But this book is intended as a small part of such a justification of 4 and many other presuppositions that traditional Christians believe.

What about option 1? Though option 1 is not held by the vast majority of Americans, it is the view that dominates the university world and is held tenaciously by many, if not most, biologists. The short form of this view is simply stated: "Evolution by solely natural, undesigned means is a fact." And one scientist has added, "It is absolutely safe to say that if you meet somebody who claims not to believe in evolution, that person is ignorant, stupid, or insane (or wicked, but I'd rather not go there)."[8]

Option 1 rests on the *autonomy of human reason*—that is, the ability of human reason on its own to discern the truth. In fact, the judgment of 1 is usually given with precisely the sense of certitude sought by Descartes. But is it so obvious? Is it so certain?

One way to question it is to see whether Neo-Darwinism actually explains what it claims to explain. This is the tack taken by design scientists, those who plump for ID (intelligent design). But that is not the tack I want to take. I want to question a more basic underlying assumption—the autonomy of human reason. I want to demonstrate that from human reason alone—reason that has emerged solely from inside human consciousness—there can be no assurance that what an individual consciousness thinks it knows is actually true.

THE AUTONOMY OF HUMAN REASON

Since the Enlightenment, the major assumption of Western philosophy has been the *autonomy of human reason*—the notion that at the foundation of all knowledge is the trustworthiness of the human intellect in general and the intellect of every individual human.

In brief, the argument, stemming from René Descartes, is this: God might not exist; the external world might not exist; but at least I must exist. To wit: *I think, therefore I am.* After all, even if what I think I am is not what I am, if I am aware I must be something. Even if I doubt that I am, I must *be* or I wouldn't be doubting. On this rests the case Descartes made for the certainty that at least he—a thinking thing—existed.

Descartes went on to analyze what made this conclusion valid, concluding that its clearness and distinctness and the impossibility of concluding otherwise guaranteed its truth. It was not necessary to bring anyone else or anything else into the picture. One could know this on one's own. Certitude of knowledge could rest not on any revelation either directly from God or indirectly from a book, but solely on human reason itself. Hence the autonomy of human reason.

There are countless variations on the notion of the autonomy of human reason. The so-called rationalists following Descartes (Leibniz, for example) privileged self-evident propositions, and the empiricists (John Locke, for example) relied on sense perception as fundamental. But the main epistemological project of philosophers from the mid-seventeenth century to the present has been to assume the autonomy of human reason. One text assigned by my first philosophy teacher—Russell's *Problems in Philosophy*—presents this view in spades.[9]

At first many philosophers were interested in demonstrating the existence of God. Descartes, for example, argued that it was necessary to show that God exists before one could be sure that the external world exists. Later philosophers, Nietzsche chief among them, took a more radical stance, rejecting as invalid any of the classic medieval or Enlightenment proofs for the existence of God.[10] The result was that human reason was cut off completely from any connection to a divine reality.

For naturalists, of course, God does not now exist, nor has he ever existed. Human reason can have no other ground than itself. So if one is to trust in human reason, it will be because human reason is somehow trustworthy and can be seen to be so by the human mind.

But is it? Critics—both atheists like Nietzsche and theists like J. P. Moreland—have long been convinced that human reason cannot ground itself. Any and all claims to the trustworthiness of the human mind rest on unproven assumptions. The acceptance of the autonomy of human reason is just as much a belief taken on faith as the notion that God exists. Indeed, some would say it is a far less justifiable belief than the belief that God exists. But this is to get ahead of my argument here.

We should first take a closer, longer look at the case for the autonomy of human reason, beginning by way of indirection.

A View from Outer Space: Stanislaw Lem

Sometimes the way into a problem is first to step back and see it from a distance. A story by Stanislaw Lem (1921–2006) can help us do that. At the same time we will see one way worldviews relate to narratives.

But first let me address the notion that though some literature is openly philosophic, literature as such is not philosophy as ordinarily understood. My argument focuses on literature that inevitably embodies philosophy and often theology.

THE LIMITS OF PHILOSOPHICAL PROSE

Literary form is not separable from philosophical content, but is, itself, a part of content—an integral part, then, of the search for and the statement of truth.

But this suggests, too, that there may be some views of the world and how one should live in it—views, especially, that emphasize the world's surprising variety, its complexity and mysteriousness, its flawed and imperfect beauty—that cannot be fully and adequately stated in the language of conventional philosophical prose, a style remarkably flat and lacking in wonder—but only in a language and in forms themselves more complex, more allusive, more attentive to particulars. Not perhaps, either, in the expositional structure conventional to philosophy, which sets out to establish something and then does so, without surprise, without incident—but only in a form that itself implies that life contains significant surprises, that our task, as agents, is to live as good characters in a good story do, caring about what happens, resourcefully confronting each new thing. If these views are serious candidates for truth, views that the search for truth ought to consider along its way, then it seems that this language and these forms ought to be included within philosophy.

—Martha Nussbaum, "Introduction: Form and Content, Philosophy and Literature," in *Love's Knowledge* (Oxford: Oxford University Press, 1990), pp. 3-4

Lem was a Polish science fiction writer whose work has been honored more on the Continent than in the United States. I will focus on an untitled episode of *The Cyberiad,* a comic epic set in the far-flung future—a future in which all the Star Trek voyages would have been lost in antiquity.[11] At the time of the action, cybernetics is all that remains of conscious life. In an untitled section I call "Mymosh the Selfbegotten," Lem recounts in a handful of pages events that take place over eons on a planet in a galaxy so far removed from Earth that it takes Lem ten lines to place its location.

Trurl, a robot who makes robots, finds himself in trouble as his spaceship encounters an odd force field. In his attempt to right the ship, he tosses out various useless items, including a broken jug. This jug, following without fault the laws of physics, hurtles through space until it crashes on top of a garbage dump on a planet on which life has long ago disappeared. Tumbling down the slope and skittering into a puddle, it sets in motion a series of electrical and mechanical events that end in producing a robot with both physical senses and logic circuits—an android. Lem calls him "Mymosh the Selfbegotten, who had neither mother nor father, but was son unto himself, for his father was Coincidence and his mother Entropy" (p. 189).

Utterly without design and poorly constructed, the robot clambers out of the puddle, takes a few steps and then looks at his reflection in the water. Lem tells us that this "purely accidental" creature, fashioned from trash, is a bundle of misshapen features and loose screws. But when he sees his reflection, he blurts out, "Truly, I am beautiful, nay, perfect, which clearly implies the Perfection of All Created Things!! Ah, and how good must be the One Who fashioned me!" Then he hobbles on, "humming hymns in praise of the Everlasting Harmony of Providence" (p. 189).

On the seventh step, however, Mymosh stumbles, falls and shorts out. His machinery rusts, and he remains unaware of his existence for 314,000 years, after which a boot flung from another spacecraft tumbles down the garbage heap and boots Mymosh back into a puddle, where his logic circuits are reactivated and he thinks "the following thought: Apparently, I am!" (p. 190). But this is all he can think for another sixteen centuries. Then, as happenstance would have it, a bird relieves itself and the droppings hit Mymosh "square on the forehead," and Mymosh speaks again: "Yes, I am! And there's no apparently about it! Yet the question remains, who is it who says that I am? Or, in other words, who am I?" (p. 190).

Mymosh doesn't know it, but in his reawakened form he has forgotten his earlier conscious existence and lost all his senses. He tries to identify other things around him but can find none. As he puts it, "I can plainly see that I see nothing whatsoever! Therefore there's only I that am, and everything that is and may be, for I can think in any way I like" (p. 190). He doesn't want to leap to this conclusion without further consideration of the possibility that something lies beyond his consciousness, but after more thought he still finds nothing to justify thinking that anything other than he himself exists. So he concludes that he is alone.

Bored with the singularity of his consciousness, Mymosh begins to create a Gozmos, a world within himself, peopling it with a variety of personal beings—Beadlies and Pratlings, for example. But they fight and give Mymosh a headache. So he creates a second Gozmos, one of "caprice and miracle." In this Gozmos "something might occur one way once, and at another time be altogether different—and without any special rhyme or reason" (p. 192).

But just as his second Gozmos is getting interesting, a fragment from Trurl's jug—now sixteen centuries old—taps Mymosh's delicate rusty skull, "and the murky water rushed in over the copper coils and extinguished the current in the logic circuits, and the Gozmos of Mymosh the Selfbegotten attained the perfection, the ultimate perfection that comes with nothingness. And those who unwittingly had brought him into the world never learned of his passing" (p. 192).

This delightful story loses much of its charm in the abridged retelling, but it still poses for us a view from the outside. What, then, do we see?

First, we must recognize that there are really two Mymoshes in the story. Mymosh One exists for only a few minutes, long enough to see himself, create an argument for the existence of God and start a religion. Not bad for a few minutes! Oh, yes, quite bad, for Mymosh One is utterly wrong at every turn. He is not perfect; his creators—coincidence and entropy—did not craft him by design; and there is no Providence to be everlastingly harmonious.

Actually, in incredibly brief compass, Lem—a naturalist, as he makes explicit in his essays—has launched a parabolic refutation of the cosmological argument for the existence of God.[12] Notice that even though he possesses both senses and the ability to reason, Mymosh One just does not

know what he is talking about. He looks, he sees, he interprets, and he leaps
to conclusions that are false.

Mymosh Two, though he exists far longer than Mymosh One, is also mistaken about who he is. Of course he has less to go on than Mymosh One; he
has lost both his senses and his memory of being Mymosh One. He can only
think. And when he does so, his first thought is an expression of a primary
intuition: "I am." He is simply self-aware, aware of his own existence.

Mymosh Two imitates the biblical Yahweh, who, when asked to give his
name, responded to Moses, "I AM WHO I AM" (Exodus 3:14). Like Yahweh,
Mymosh Two doesn't argue about whether he is. He just asserts that he is.
Unlike Descartes (as we will see), Mymosh Two doesn't first try to doubt that
he is, then conclude that doubting implies his own existence. He simply
intuits himself to be a self, an "I" that is.

Later he indulges in a kind of Cartesian doubt. He looks again, trying to
"see" whether in fact there isn't someone or something else, but, because he
has no senses, he sees no one. He then feels guilty for even trying. For an
only "god" not to be intuitively certain of its own singular existence makes
it less of a god than it should be. That might have given Mymosh Two a clue
that he might not be alone. Mymosh Two might have recognized that a
sense of guilt implies a standard outside oneself. That would be an Other.
If he feels guilty, maybe there is an Other. But Mymosh Two does not
tumble to this hint.

Both Mymosh One and Mymosh Two make serious mistakes about who
they are. Why?

Mymosh One and Mymosh Two mistake who they are for two simple
reasons: they do not have enough information, and they have no way of
getting it. They are part of a story that is larger than themselves—larger than
all of our stories. There is a vast cosmos out there beyond the Mymoshes. It
runs on coincidence and entropy—chance (the peculiar facticity or mani-
festation of a universe that expands in one specific way rather than another
but does so without purpose) and necessity (the physical laws of the universe), Jacques Monod would say.[13]

Mymosh One is conscious of himself (as beautiful!) and of some of what
is outside himself, but he reasons from at least one false premise (that he is
perfect), and so his conclusion is false. He creates a story in which he fits,

but the story is false. Mymosh Two is locked inside his own consciousness. He hasn't a clue to the larger story in which he fits. So, god of his own godhood, he makes up his own story, one that comes to an untimely end as the larger story encompasses his.

How as readers do we know this? We know it because Lem—the creator-god of *The Cyberiad*—tells us. The universe of *The Cyberiad* is the universe of Lem's imagination. It is what I will call a Secondary World in chapter three below. If Lem, its creator, tells us, we can know about it.

Here, then, lies a clue to the search for our own identity. If we—as finite beings, let alone as fallen ones—are to know who we really are, we will have to be told. Like Mymosh One, we have senses and reason, but we have no assurance solely within ourselves that we have access to enough information to identify ourselves accurately. We need an author who is willing to tell us something about the story in which we are characters. If there is such an author, we have hope. We might not have philosophic certitude (what Descartes was searching for). But we would have reason to believe that some of our self-knowledge is true. And if there were some reason to believe that there is such an author, we would have some justification for believing the story itself.

There is a deep irony in Lem's story. Lem himself, like Richard Dawkins, believes that there is no one outside us to tell us what the master story of the universe is. In a serious essay on the history of the universe, Lem says, "To put the matter most concisely: the hypotheses that reconstruct the past ten billion years of the Milky Way's existence tell us that man emerged because the Universe is a place of catastrophe; that Earth, together with life, owes its existence to a peculiar sequence of catastrophes."[14] The human implications of this naturalist master story are tragic: "Where there is No One—therefore no feelings, friendly or hostile, no love or hate—there are also no intentions. The Universe, being neither a Person nor the work of any Person, cannot be accused of bias in its action: it simply is what it is and does what it does."[15]

Human beings, Lem admits, are shut off from any ability to know with any assurance the master story of the universe. Every "ultimate view of reality," he says, is suspect. His only hope is in a more-than-human technology: "It may be that someday a *deus ex machina* will cope with these inhuman, over complicated measurements, inaccessible to our poor animal brains: alienated, human-initiated machine intelligence—or, rather, the product, pretermechanical, of a human-launched evolution of synthetic mind. But here I overstep the twenty-first century into a darkness that no speculation can illumine."[16]

Give Lem credit. He does not imagine in his science fiction novels any such "synthetic mind." But note, nonetheless, that Lem's own story of Mymosh the Selfbegotten contains the seeds of its own deconstruction. The reason we know Mymosh One and Mymosh Two are mistaken about who they are is that there is an omnipotent narrator—Lem the author—who constructs the universe, the Secondary World, of the story. This universe "imitates" in its character the universe Lem thinks actually exists—a universe of chance and entropy. But in such a universe, all human beings—you and I and Lem too—are Mymoshes. What we think we know, we know by virtue of our finite senses and reason. In such a universe, we could be just as misled by our senses and reason as was Mymosh One. Why is Lem so sure that we are in a universe that is controlled by chance and entropy? Maybe Mymosh One was right after all. It just depends on what the master story is, whether someone wrote it intentionally and whether the author will tell us.

So to the moral of the story: (1) naturalism does not give us a foundation for trusting our senses and our reason, (2) if naturalism is true, we can have little assurance that it is true, and (3) most important, we can have no assurance that our seeming knowledge of our own "self" is true.[17]

DESCARTES REVISITED

If Lem's story has not misled us, then we can conclude this: if there is no "god" to ground our reason, then there is no reason to accept the results of our reason. But perhaps Lem's story has missed something. Let's look again at Descartes's argument, this time in more detail.[18]

It may surprise us to learn that Augustine (A.D. 354–430) had considered and used a form of the "cogito" argument (I think; therefore I am) centuries before as he turned his attention to the inner workings of the mind. But until René Descartes (1596–1650), no one examined the "proto-cogito" and asked what it implied about the self itself. In doing this Descartes became the first "modern" philosopher, the first philosopher to take epistemology as a "first thing" for thought. For previous philosophers from the pre-

Socratics to Descartes, including Augustine, the main starting point was the recognition that there is something outside oneself. The question was, what is it? In other words, metaphysics (the study of what is there), not epistemology (the study of how we know what is there), was the fundamental discipline, the "first thing."

In Christian theology this was true as well. The term *theology* itself betrays its nature: theology is the study of God (*theo*), not the study of how we know God is God (epistemology), not the study of revelation (biblical theology), not the study of how we understand the nature of revelation (hermeneutics). These other studies were all there in some form, but none of them was a "first thing."

With Descartes, the focus shifted from *what* is there to how *I* can be *certain* that what *I think* is there is in fact there. Attendant on this is the question of what or who it is that "thinks." We enter the world of modern philosophy the moment we reach this passage in Descartes's *Meditations*: "I do not now admit anything which is not necessarily true: to speak accurately, I am not more than a thing which thinks, that is to say a mind or a soul, or an understanding, or a reason, which are terms whose significance was formerly unknown to me. I am, however, a real thing and really exist; what thing? I have answered: a thing which thinks."[19]

Here is the essence of the modern: one individual person, on the foundation of his own autonomy, declaring that he knows with philosophic (i.e., justified) certainty that he or she is a thinking thing. Descartes then rests all of his philosophy on this foundation.[20] This fateful move sets the agenda for modern philosophy from Locke to Kant and sparks the recoil of postmodern philosophy from Nietzsche to Derrida.

In the Western world, all of us born after the seventeenth century inherit the predilection of Western culture to begin (and often to end) our thoughts and our search for truth with ourselves. "I can make up my own mind. Who are you to tell me what to believe? It's true for me. It doesn't have to be true for you. My truth is my truth." Comments like these, heard now on the streets and in the universities of every major city in the world, have their roots in the seventeenth century, in particular in the philosophy of Descartes.

What I have come to believe, however, is this. The human mind is curious about many matters that are far beyond its capacity to encompass. We try to understand God—the finite attempts to encompass the infinite. But this is impossible. Nevertheless, the Enlightenment, following the direction set by Descartes, assumed the autonomy and sufficiency of human reason. Human reason is all we have to understand reality, and it is enough. Okay, so we don't yet know the answers to all our questions.

THE DEEP DISQUIET OF THE RESTLESS HEART

We have been taught not only to see the physical order as no more than mindless machinery, but also to believe (or to suspect) that this machinery is all there is. Our metaphysical imagination now makes it seem quite reasonable to conclude that the deep disquiet of the restless heart that longs for God is not in fact a rational appetite that can be sated by any real object, but only a mechanical malfunction in need of correction. . . . Perhaps what we require to be free from illusion is not escape to some higher realm, but only reparation of the psyche, reintegration of the unconscious and the ego, reconciliation with ourselves—in a word, therapy.

Dominant ideologies wither away, metaphysical myths exhaust their power to hold sway over cultural imaginations, material and spiritual conditions change inexorably and irreversibly. The human longing for God, however, persists from age to age. A particular cultural dispensation may succeed for a time in lulling the soul into a forgetful sleep, but the soul will still continue to hear that timeless call that comes at once from within and from beyond all things, even if for now it seems like only a voice heard in a dream. And, sooner or later, the sleeper will awaken.

—David Bentley Hart, "Jung's Therapeutic Gnosticism," review of Carl Jung's *Red Book, First Things,* January 2013, pp. 30-31

We can take this chastened confidence in human reason either as good news (as did the Enlightenment or the modernists and the optimistic postmodernists) or as bad news (as did the nihilists and the pessimistic postmodernists). The reasoning in both cases is still viciously circular. Autonomous human reason tells us human reason is autonomous;

therefore human reason is autonomous.

This Enlightenment, however, was a great Darkening. Enlightenment intellectuals and their progeny have cut themselves off both from the wisdom of the past (the great books of the Western and Eastern worlds) and, much more seriously, from the revelation from God found in Scripture. If God is as infinite as we humans (traditional Christians and others) assume, he will have to tell us who he is. And we find that he has done that in the Old and New Testaments.

For now, we are back to zero. From what beginning will we as Christians build our grasp of God, humans and the cosmos? Will it be the autonomy of human reason or the wisdom of the ancients, most notably the Old and New Testaments taken as the revelation from the infinite-personal God? Both require some sort of commitment. Viewed from our individual or even Christian corporate standpoint, neither of them can be proved. Every argument must start from somewhere taken as the "beginning." Where will we begin, if not from inside the box?

The answer is good news. There is a beginning deeper than human reason. Christians usually call that deeper perception *faith* or, as Bernard Ramm does, *the testimonium* or the witness of the Holy Spirit.[21] If I were doing typical epistemology, I would be quite willing to use those terms, but there is another way to describe what is really happening in the human heart and mind. It's my fourth explanation for confidence not so much in human reason as in direct perception—the sort of intuitive seeing that is not unreasonable but beyond reason. An audacious claim? Yes—but one that is also quite biblical. That's the subject of the next chapter.

3

IN THE BEGINNING

An Argument from God

> ◆ <

In the beginning God created the heavens and the earth.

Genesis 1:1

In the previous chapter we reached an impasse. The assumption of the autonomy of human reason—implicit or explicit—leads to a dead end. It's nihilism in disguise, or as Helmut Thielicke might say, "ciphered nihilism."[1] I well know that this accusation is not acceptable to many thoughtful naturalists. They insist that human reason may not be perfect but that it works well in daily life and, more importantly, in science. And with science that's enough. My friend Carl, who worked for years as a biochemist in cancer research, bristles when I try to convince him that his confidence in human reason is really nihilism in disguise.[2]

After years of wrangling and reflecting on this impasse, I've come to the conclusion that Carl dismisses my arguments primarily because he is dead set against there being a God to whom he might be responsible. Except for his refusal to admit it, I think Carl is a lot like philosopher Thomas Nagel: "I want atheism to be true and am made uneasy by the fact that some of the most intelligent and well-informed people I know are religious believers. It isn't just that I don't believe in God and, naturally, hope that I'm right in my belief. It's that I hope there is no God! I don't want there to be a God; I don't want the universe to be like that."[3]

A SENSE OF DEITY

That there exists in the human mind, and indeed by natural instinct, some sense of Deity, we hold to be beyond dispute, since God himself, to prevent any man from pretending ignorance, has endued all men with some idea of his Godhead, the memory of which he constantly renews and occasionally enlarges, that all to a man, being aware that there is a God, and that he is their Maker, may be condemned by their own conscience when they neither worship him nor consecrate their lives to his service. . . . Since, then, there never has been, from the very first, any quarter of the globe, any city, any household even, without religion, this amounts to a tacit confession, that a sense of Deity is inscribed on every heart. . . .

All men of sound judgment will therefore hold, that a sense of Deity is indelibly engraven on the human heart. And that this belief is naturally engendered in all, and thoroughly fixed as it were in our very bones, is strikingly attested by the contumacy of the wicked, who, though they struggle furiously, are unable to extricate themselves from the fear of God. Though Diagoras, and others of like stamp, make themselves merry with whatever has been believed in all ages concerning religion, and Dionysius scoffs at the judgment of heaven, it is but a Sardonian grin; for the worm of conscience, keener than burning steel, is gnawing them within.

—John Calvin, *Institutes of the Christian Religion,* trans. Henry Beveridge (London: James Clark, n.d.), 1.3.1 and 3

Of course, my response to Carl is not a strictly rational criticism. My claim is that he has replaced a desire for truth with a will to sustain his own autonomy in spite of *reality.* That is an even more serious charge. In fact it seems to belie Aristotle's opening statement in his *Metaphysics*: "All people desire to know." One of our unique human tendencies—many would say—is to seek truth wherever it can be found, no matter how pleasant or unpleasant it is. The problem is not that those who argue against the God of the Bible do not desire knowledge of the truth; it's that they exchange the truth of God for something they think more reasonable—that is much more palatable to a sinner trying to explain away the God whose lordship they have no desire to acknowledge. Pointing this out to a committed naturalist will almost certainly carry no weight with him or her. This is obvious from Carl's closing remarks in *Deepest Differences*.[4] But it is something to keep in mind as we confront those who easily dismiss God's existence.

Many atheists are in fact not willing to see such fundamental realities that belong to the truth they believe they are seeking. But many of those who believe God exists may be doing so for the same reason—they want God to exist and will believe he does in spite of any counterevidence or counterargument they confront. In any case, when we as Christians present a thoughtful case for our faith in Christ, we should refrain from charging—or even assuming—that our interlocutor is being any less intellectually honest than we are.

So what reasons other than their desire for God not to exist do atheists cite? First, some insist that there is little or no empirical evidence for God. This any believer in God will find very odd. As Calvin wrote: "God's essence, indeed, is incomprehensible, utterly transcending all human thought; but on each of his works his glory is engraven in characters so bright, so distinct, and so illustrious, that none, however dull and illiterate, can plead ignorance as their excuse."[5] Moreover, there are many rational arguments that begin with empirical data and argue toward God's existence—arguments from historical data leading to a forceful case for the resurrection of Jesus, arguments from the makeup of material reality (the complexity of DNA, for example), arguments from the observable character of the cosmos. The "lack of evidence" charge is quite simply bogus. Or is that also name calling? Let's say it does not stand fair analysis. And there is a library of books to back up this claim.

Second, some atheists reject the existence of the Christian notion of God for abstract logical reasons. For example, if God were the perfect being Christians believe he is, he wouldn't have created the present obviously imperfect world. Arguments of this sort have been assessed by Christians and found invalid, or at least less than convincing.[6]

Third, some atheists argue that the various scientific methods used to discover the nature of the material universe neither require nor assume the existence of God or any other ex nihilo creator. That is correct. The problem, rather, is that science relies on the autonomy of human reason, and as we have seen in the previous chapter, that reliance is problematic. Consider the following dystopian vision.

All the methodologies of natural science assume that the human mind as represented by the community of scientists is capable of reaching or approaching (closer and closer) to the truth about the natural world. The scientific community investigates, considers, reasons, evaluates, makes hypotheses (some looking reasonable, some looking wildly radical, impossible, "clearly" wrong, which are confined to the dustbin or eventually accepted by the bulk of the scientific community as brilliantly imaginative grasps of truth). The autonomous mind checks the accuracy of the autonomous mind, like bank managers who audit their own banks. In the imagery of Stanislaw Lem, the Mymosh scientific community constructs an imaginary world of scientific understanding, never suspecting that outside the community of (human) reason there exists another transnatural world that has provided the machinery that has generated this magnificent world of (human) science. This is a world that disappears in a nanosecond as the mind of that world, by whim or design, attains "the ultimate perfection that comes with nothingness," and the vast company of men and women, scientists and philosophers, who worked in the imagined world "never learns of its passing."

THE CHRISTIAN DIFFERENCE

Christians, however, do not have to assume on the basis of human reason alone that human reason is trustworthy. For Christians, confidence in human reason rests on its being rooted in a God who fashions human reason to lead to truth. As God is the all-knowing knower of all things, we, being made in his image, can be the sometimes knowing knowers of some things—things that are sufficient for us to know. That may not satisfy our curiosity, but it's good enough.

But wait. Let's look again. Are we Christians on any better footing than naturalists? Isn't our argument just as circular? No, even though at first it may appear so. Christians ultimately know that human reason can lead to the discovery of truths about reality because God made them able to know. This gives a reason for human reason that is not based on human reason alone but on the existence of a God who made humans capable of using their mind and body to discover some truth about both the natural and the supernatural world. In other words, for an atheist reason is a self-attesting given; for Christians reason is a God-attesting gift. A properly Christian epistemology is not justified by an epistemology but by an ontology. The first question should not be "How can anyone know that Christianity is true?" Rather, the first question that matters is "What is the fundamental truth about reality?" Or "What *is* the really real?"[7]

THE TRANSCENDENT DISPELLED

The metaphysical picture of reality that the West has embraced ever more unreflectively since the rise of a mechanistic philosophy of nature is one that forcibly expels the transcendent from the immanent. At one time, it seemed enough simply to open one's eyes to see the light of the divine reflected in the mirror of creation: The cosmos was everywhere the work of formal and final causes and of a pervasive divine wisdom, an endlessly diverse but harmonious *scala naturae* rising up from the earth to heaven. The whole universe was a kind of theophany, and all of reality participated in those transcendental perfections that had their infinite consummation in God. Now, however, we have learned, generation after generation, to see nature as only a machine, composed of material forces that are inherently mindless, intrinsically devoid of purpose, and therefore only adventitiously and accidentally directed towards any end, either by chance or by the hand of some demiurgic "Intelligent Designer."

—David Bentley Hart, "Jung's Therapeutic Gnosticism," review of Carl Jung's *Red Book, First Things,* January 2013, p. 29

Here is a Christian response in a bit more detail. It is an argument from *being*—from ontology, from "what is." It does not start from the thinker, the "I" of Decartes's "therefore." It does not start from the knower or the knowing but from the reality that is there to be known. It starts from the ultimate reality. God himself—not just abstract Being but the self-existent Trinity, the Father, the Son and the Holy Spirit, the Creator who has revealed himself in Jesus Christ.

As human beings, whether we know it or not, we live in the world—the cosmos—of God's creation. From God's own infinite goodness, intelligence and creativity, God fashioned our material, intelligent, moral and creative human being. We *are* because he *is.* This is our fundamental situation as human beings. This is where we are. And because we are here, because this is what really is, we begin any rational or emotional case we make for the truth of the Christian faith standing on a Rock. No, not a Rock, and not standing. Rather, we make our case for Christian faith immersed in the immanence of the transcendent God—the personal God who becomes known in a single Palestinian Jewish man; the very God who spoke all things into existence yet likes to present himself through water, bread and wine; the God of the Milky Way and the old rugged cross.

And what a glorious irony! The atheist as well as the Christian is surrounded, penetrated, permeated with the presence of this God. We can and should come to sense his concretely revealed character in all things—yes, all things, as they are now, the beautiful and the ugly, the good and the bad, the new and the old, in life and in imagined story, in prose and in poetry.

This presence of God is the foundation for all rational arguments. We do not rest our case for either our existence or our understanding on our self-perception, our recognition that I or we are (that we exist). We simply *are,* and we begin, then, with what we are.

We are intelligent and can reason and know because God made it possible for us to do so. We have the moral capacity to understand the difference between right and wrong for the same reason. We are made that way.[8] Indeed, we are made in God's image (Genesis 1:27).

So what are we? In short, we are created beings, made like God in our personality, our intelligence, our moral sensitivity, our creativity. Our social character is grounded in God, for our Creator, the Trinity, is likewise social; the one and many of creation, its endlessly fascinating diversity and unity, is rooted in the One and Three of the Trinity.

When we think, when we set out to argue, when we make a case for the truth we hold as Christians, we can do so in confidence. We are not arguing in a circle. We are immersed in God, who knows himself perfectly and faithfully gives himself to be known. Fallen and finite as we are, we can be confident that we can know some of the truth about who we are, what the universe is and, of course, who the God is in whose final reality we are immersed—so that we can finally understand not simply what exists but what it *means.*

Still, a skeptic might say, your story may seem all well and good for you, but how can you be so confident that God is there, here, everywhere? You've told a fantastic story. You are simply Mymosh Three imagining a universe of your own making. Just wait till a shard from Trurl's jug touches your circuits and you attain the "perfection that comes from nothingness"!

Yes, it would be fantastic were it not for one—again—primary fact. Christians are not Mymoshes, creatures resulting solely from the workings of the material universe that banged from nothing—at least nothing we can name. Our belief in God doesn't establish his reality, but his reality establishes our belief.

We know who we are because the transcendent God has been immanent in his creation from its very beginning. You see, "long ago God spoke to our ancestors in many and various ways by the prophets, but in these last days he has spoken to us by a Son, whom he appointed heir of all things, through whom he also created the worlds" (Hebrews 1:1-2).

Lem the creator of Mymosh One and Mymosh Two did not tell his creation who he is. He told *us.* And the story itself, despite Lem's seeming lack of grasping this, tells us that such a creature as Mymosh—one brought into being as described by, say, Richard Dawkins—is totally unequipped to understand either who he really is or what his surrounding world is.

A Christian's worldview is, therefore, supported by revelation from outside (yet within) the box of the material cosmos. A personal God has wanted us to know who we are, how we have come to be as we are and where our lives are leading. We are not trapped inside the material cosmos; we are not bound by the whims of self-attesting reason; we have a transcendent source for our being and for our knowledge of who we are.

Still, the skeptic may say, "Okay, your story makes sense and is coherent. But is there any material or logical *evidence* that this story is really true?" This, then, is where epistemology enters in—even for those, like me, who insist that ontology is primary. There is, indeed, a role for Christian apologetics.

There are several ways to respond—enough ways to make the process messy, but enough core elements to bring us through the confusion to a confident commitment to Christian faith. The following is a three-pronged apologetic approach to evidential argument based on the reality of God.

1. *An argument from God, not to God.* This is the story told in the Bible, the story of a God who creates, sustains and brings the cosmos to its glorious end. I've summarized it above. Like Lem telling us that Mymosh One and Mymosh Two are creatures brought into being by entropy and coincidence, the Bible tells us about the transcendent and immanent personal Creator of the universe, human beings and their role in God's plan.

Since the story of who we are comes through the Bible, we can study it and examine its multiple claims. Where they can be checked, do they hold up? Where they cannot be checked, are they consistent with those that can be checked? Libraries are full of the works of scholars who have done, and are continuing to do, this. See the bibliography at the end of this book.

2. *An argument from everything to God.* This argument begins in the next chapter and focuses on literature.

3. *An argument from our personal experience—direct perception—of God* in *everything.* This argument begins now.

SIGNALS OF TRANSCENDENCE

What happens when we first perceive something? Well, that's easy: something must be there. Okay, so what is it?

Imagine a baby's first observations. Her experience is raw; only gradually do babies identify what they perceive as, say, breast, mama, blanket and on and on till they can attach names to their perception and verbs that make sentences. Eventually, they come to understand their world in the language of their world, then their shared world and eventually their own identity in that world.

At first there is little or no self-referential thought. The baby does not say either "It is" or "I am." Both take time to develop, and they do as the baby grows to adulthood. Children's inner world is shaped by their outer world in ways that their inner world is not aware of. Sometimes their inner world gets interested in matters that transcend the natural world. My daughter Carol, when she was about five years old, asked her mother where God is. They were in the kitchen at the time.

"Everywhere," her mother replied.

"Is he in the bedroom?"

"Yes."

"Is he in the living room?"

"Yes."

"Is he here in the kitchen?"

"Yes."

Carol looked around the room, down at her feet, then up at her mother, eyes wide with wonder. "Am I stepping on God?"

Our conscious world does not contain the answer her mother gave, but my daughter was asking the key question of all: what, or, much better, *who*, is really there? Carol had a primitive perception of the transcendent, personal God of biblical theism. That perception was immediate, direct, palpable.[9] It had, no doubt, been prepared for by her Christian environment, but the perception was also really hers.

May I be so bold as to say that my daughter had just incarnated the words of the apostle Paul: "Ever since the creation of the world [God's] eternal power and divine nature, invisible though they are, have been understood and seen through the things he has made" (Romans 1:20).

As ordinary human beings, we perceive many things, and some of them lead us to wonder and question and pursue explanations. Some of these explanations involve more than the natural world. Here are a few that have intrigued us and triggered more than natural explanations.[10]

Blaise Pascal points to the ambivalence of human nature—its glory and its wretchedness—arguing that this is best explained by our creation in the image of God and our subsequent rebellion against him. Francis Schaeffer echoes this, speaking of the "mannishness of man." Many apologists consider features in the cosmos—for example, the fine-tuning of its physical constants.[11]

Peter Berger identifies five elements of ordinary life that operate as "signals of transcendence."[12] First is the argument from ordering, one demonstration of which is the calming love of a mother for her child terrified in the night. Against all prospect that the child's life along with her own will never end, a mother says, "There, there. It's all right. Everything is all right." That can only be true if there is more to reality than the material. "Every parent (or at any rate, every parent who loves his child) takes upon himself the representation of a universe that is ultimately in order and ultimately trustworthy. This representation can be justified only within a religious (strictly speaking, a supernatural) frame of reference."[13]

Second is the argument from play. Play takes place in a "Secondary World" with its own rules, its own order; time is suspended; eternity is assumed.

Third is the argument from hope. From birth to death we live in hope of a future, one that is challenged by suffering and death but not conquered, for we project our lives out into eternity and see beyond for a satisfaction of our longings.

Fourth is the argument from damnation. Some things we see are so despicable, so inconceivably horrible, so damnable, that in our hearts we curse the perpetrators. Only eternal banishment of the perpetrator from God and the human community seems appropriate.[14]

Berger's fifth argument is the argument from humor. In humor there are two claims, each vying for authority; which is the reality, which the transcendent? That is, humor results when what is expected is replaced by something unexpected but nonetheless possible. Another world of discourse exists beside the expected one, surprisingly transcending it. Both worlds exist at the same time, as does a world that embodies the presence of the Other.[15]

In my memoir *The Rim of the Sandhills* I have pointed to events in my life on the ranch—three thunderheads that appeared to me as the Father, the Son and the Holy Ghost; the salvation of our herd of Herefords from the spring floodwaters, the sense of God's presence in congregational prayer, and a sudden fainting as I wrestled with my decision to accept Christ as Savior and Lord.

In the chapters that follow I will discuss signals of transcendence in literature. These are found in the work of not only the profoundly Christian Gerald Manley Hopkins but also the skeptic Emily Dickinson, the nihilist Stephen Crane and the Buddhist Matsuo Bashō.[16] I will also point to works of art by Ben Shahn, Francisco Goya, and Zen Buddhist monks. Finally, I will point to the One who ties all these together and reveals himself in Jesus Christ.[17]

These signals of transcendence are not so much arguments for Christian faith as ontological elements of reality itself standing in front of each of us and saying, "Look at me. Don't you see? I cannot be what you see me to be if there is no world beyond your own."[18]

John Hundley, a recent graduate in religious studies, recognizes this as he looks with "a new critical eye" at the world before him: "I started to see with my own mind and heart that everything in the universe, physical or not, beckons with a long arm and points the weary-eyed traveler toward a God of rest and love, justice and order, reason and work."[19]

NONE CAN PLEAD IGNORANCE

Since the perfection of blessedness consists in the knowledge of God [John 17:3] he has been pleased, in order that none might be excluded from the means of obtaining felicity, not only to deposit in our minds that seed of religion of which we have already spoken, but so to manifest his perfections in the whole structure of the universe, and daily place himself in our view, that we cannot open our eyes without being compelled to behold him. His essence, indeed, is incomprehensible, utterly transcending all human thought; but on each of his works his glory is engraven in characters so bright, so distinct, and so illustrious, that none, however dull and illiterate, can plead ignorance as their excuse. Hence, with perfect truth, the Psalmist exclaims, "He covereth himself with light as with a garment" [Psalm 104:2], as if he had said, that God for the first time was arrayed in visible attire when, in the creation of the world, he displayed those glorious banners, on which, to whatever side we turn, we behold his perfections visibly portrayed. In the same place, the Psalmist aptly compares the expanded heavens to his royal tent, and says, "He layeth the beams of his chambers in the waters, maketh the clouds his chariot, and walketh upon the wings of the wind," sending forth the winds and lightnings as his swift messengers. And because the glory of his power and wisdom is more refulgent in the firmament, it is frequently designated as his palace. And, first, wherever you turn your eyes, there is no portion of the world, however minute, that does not exhibit at least some sparks of beauty; while it is impossible to contemplate the vast and beautiful fabric as it extends around, without being overwhelmed by the immense weight of glory.

—John Calvin, *Institutes of the Christian Religion,* trans. Henry Beveridge (London: James Clark, n.d.), 1.5.1

Signals of transcendence can be given deistic, naturalistic, pantheistic, Buddhist, even nihilistic explanations. But in the final analysis these explanations fail to account adequately for what they claim to account for. Deistic explanations cannot account for the sense that something personal is being sensed. Naturalistic explanations don't explain why human beings always act as if some acts are morally wrong, not just by one's own or one's community standards but in relation to goodness itself—a reality existing outside the nexus of material cause and effect, a reality assumed by the very perception of the difference between that which is and that which ought to be. Pantheism likewise cannot deal with the genuine difference between good and evil—a difference felt by pantheists who reflect, but not by those who engage in meditative techniques that shut down the human faculty of attention to reality. Nihilistic explanations are self-refuting, and Buddhist explanations deny the reality of the experience itself. Only a full-blown Christian theism accounts for what Rudolf Otto identifies as the numinous and the *mysterium tremendum*.[20]

There is in all these signals of transcendence a dimension that cries out— sometimes literally, as in the great poems by Hopkins—as we shall see in the following chapter: "*I*—the phenomenon itself—exist only because there is One who has created me and in whom I live and have my being." I exist because "the world is charged with the grandeur of God . . . [and] the Holy Ghost over the bent / World broods with warm breast and with ah! bright wings." In other words, I exist only because I am brought into being and held there by an Other who transcends the material world.

GOD IN THE BEGINNING

In the beginning, God! What more profound words have ever been spoken? I can think of only one: "I AM." And this was spoken not only in the beginning but in the history of humankind. The transcendent becomes immanent in the speech recorded by the prophets. Then the very Word himself, spoken by the Father, becomes incarnate. And in him all things really do hold together—including those signals of transcendence that come in "many daily forms,"[21] among them literature and the transcendent worlds that writers create. Thus the next chapter.

4

SECONDARY WORLDS

An Argument from Literary Theory

> ◆ <

[The story-maker] makes a Secondary World which your mind can enter.
Inside it, what he relates is "true": it accords with the laws of that world.
You therefore believe it, while you are, as it were, inside. The moment
disbelief arises, the spell is broken; the magic, or rather art, has failed.
You are then out in the Primary World again, looking at the
little abortive Secondary World from outside.

J. R. R. TOLKIEN, "ON FAIRY-STORIES"

BACK TO MY STORY. Literature has been for me a major signal of transcendence. But for many years I did not see it as such. I have only done so in the past few years. When I was a child, it was only a joy, a way to spend hours and hours with books from the small shelf in our one-classroom, two-small-coatroom country schoolhouse, standing in the corner of a farmer's field almost three miles from my family's ranch. That shelf provided a dozen or so novels, classics of American literature. I remember especially *The Last of the Mohicans* by James Fenimore Cooper and *Twenty Thousand Leagues Under the Sea* by Jules Verne. Then at home I had *Jack and Jill*, a children's journal, and my parents' magazines, the *Saturday Evening Post* and *Collier's*. They carried stories about Tugboat Annie and Alexander Botts, who sold

Earthworm Tractors, and they published serials touting the deeds of valor of Horatio Hornblower.

In all these I was whisked from a farm and school with no electricity, running water or telephones to a glorious dreamland. No, I was not "uplifted into the regions of northern sky," as was C. S. Lewis as he read of Balder in *Tegner's Drapa*. Nor did I well up with Joy, that "unsatisfied desire which itself is more desirable than any other satisfaction."[2] But I could envision another world—a world beyond farming and ranching and a place where I could live in my imagination, a world beyond and above my present world, a sort of universe next door, though I would never have thought to call it that.

The study of chemistry attracted me from kindergarten through college, but when I realized that I could never do the math involved in science, I turned easily and quickly to literature. As a sophomore at the University of Nebraska, I entered again the worlds of imagination that had given me great pleasure as a child, and I encountered an issue that had puzzled me for some time. How did all this non-Christian literature I was now intently reading relate to my Christian faith?

It took years of pondering the relationship between literature and Christianity before I came to a view of literature that squares with both my faith and my experience of literature itself. What is literature? Does good literature have to tell the truth according to the Christian faith? Why do I admire the works of such writers as Albert Camus, Dylan Thomas, Sylvia Plath and Gary Snyder, clearly writers who do not confess a Christian faith?

Why have these questions intrigued me? The answer involves my individual nature—my personality and temperament—that emerged and developed as I grew. The story of that is a mystery beyond my unraveling. But I can say this.

The Christian religion and my faith within its wide, wide boundaries were always in focus in the near background. If literature other than the Bible was so intriguing as to draw me to it, then how did it and my faith intersect, especially since much of the literature that captured my attention was either oblivious to Christianity, called it into mild or serious criticism or was dead set against it? I finally encountered a clue when I studied Renaissance literature under the tutelage of Professor Donald Clark at the University of Missouri. He introduced me to worldview thinking.

Eventually, I came to a settled conviction that worldview analysis sheds light on these questions. From the concept of worldview, a study of literary criticism and a reading of vast quantities of literature from across the world and across all ages emerged my basic understanding of literature and its relation to my Christian faith. The present chapter, then, presents a theory (if that is not too pretentious) of literature. The following two chapters explain why literature itself—whether written from a Christian standpoint or not—testifies to the existence of a transcendent realm—often, in fact, to the truth of the Christian faith.

A THEORY OF LITERATURE

This theory of literature is not cut out of whole cloth. No theory is or should be. The history of literary theory is full of fascinating speculation, brilliant insights and imaginative leaps of perception—and, recently, a bit of foolishness too. Mine is a blend of themes from a variety of sources from Plato to the present, but mostly from Sir Philip Sidney, Samuel Taylor Coleridge, Joseph Conrad, James Orr, Abraham Kuyper, C. S. Lewis, J. R. R. Tolkien, E. M. W. Tillyard, Arthur O. Lovejoy, Basil Willey, René Wellek, Austin Warren, M. H. Abrams, Cleanth Brooks, Robert Penn Warren and Jacques Maritain. I won't try to sort out how these come together. I doubt that I could do it if I tried. But I can state my own theory, if in its simplicity it should be called such.

When I was a graduate student at Washington State College (now University), the New Critics Cleanth Brooks and Robert Penn Warren emphasized the primarily aesthetic dimension of literature. "A poem should not mean / But be," concluded the poet Archibald MacLeish in "Ars Poetica." Literature is on its own aesthetically detached from any sort of meaning—metaphysical or theological. In saying this MacLeish is probably playing with his readers, for he must know that he has just contradicted himself. Just as the sentence "This is not a sentence" denies itself, MacLeish's own poem denies what it says. Still, in the 1960s this line became a presupposition of many graduate students in English literature—including me.

Unfortunately, the proposition stood in the way of my seeing what most readers never doubted—that good literature is always more than objet d'art. Rather, good literature displays multiple examples of our human understandings of God, the universe and ourselves. Fortunately, long before I began my doctoral dissertation I became disabused of my earlier narrow notion of literature.

The dissertation itself ("Miltonic Criticism and the Problem of the Reader's Belief") shifts the usual attention of critics from the text itself to how its artistry is evaluated by critics with differing worldviews. Then, my own postdoctoral scholarship on the influence of Plotinus on seventeenth-century literary criticism was mostly a vision utterly unrealized. Moreover, it homed in more on philosophy, theology and worldview analysis than it did on the new moves in critical theory from Lévi-Strauss through Derrida.

For good or ill, then, in what follows you will find no influence of deconstruction or postdeconstruction or any touch of the sociopsychological orientation of feminism, Marxism and gender study. There is, as well, little hint of the hermeneutic of suspicion. I trust writers worth reading to be basically honest. I have no interest in subliminal trickery.[3] Of course, if any postmodern critical theory is itself a part of a piece of literature, it will emerge in the application of the theory I present. In short, my theory is my own blend of aesthetics, traditional Christian theology, philosophy and worldview analysis. Alas, a poor thing, but mine own.[4]

LITERATURE DEFINED

Let's start with a definition of literature as such:

> Literature is the embodiment of (1) a view of reality (2) captured in concrete terms and given (3) a linguistic structure that is appropriate to the various ideas and attitudes that make up the view of reality and that will evoke (4) an appropriate aesthetic experience in the skilled reader.

Just how this definition is Christian may not first be apparent, but I am convinced that it is Christian and that it provides a basis for understanding the relationship of all literature to the Christian faith. Let me explain.

First, literature embodies a view of reality—that is, a worldview. The particular worldview embodied in a piece of literature may not look or be very complex. How big a view of reality can a poet pack into a short lyric? More than you might imagine. Take Bashō's seventeen-syllable (in Japanese) haiku:[5]

An ancient pond
A frog leaps in
The sound of water

A skilled reader can reap from this a profound intellectual grasp and emotional feel for Bashō's non-intellectual Zen worldview. I have tried to explain this in *Naming the Elephant* and so won't go into detail here. But note this: The poem is an image set in motion but signifying motionlessness. There is an ancient pond—a legacy of the passage of time. There is a frog—an element of the present. And there is the interface between the two that negates the presence of both the past and the present, and signifies the absence of the future as well. For when the frog enters the water (a motion), it brings the past together with the present, but it creates only the sound of water. It does not go "plop" or "bloop," and certainly not "splash."[6] Rather, it makes "the sound of water"—that is, it makes no sound at all, for in the Japanese the word for sound of water is not onomatopoetic; it is just the phrase *sound of water.* Water in the present makes no sound. In the Zen conception of reality, the "really real," the fundamental character of the way things are is so utterly unspeakable and unknowable that it cannot be spoken of at all. One can only approach a grasp of what it is by seeing that it *isn't* in any sense of the word *is*. Being is nonbeing. Satori, illumination, is the experience of grasping that. This illumination takes place in the same kind of dimensionless, timeless moment that characterizes the frog's silent entry into the ancient pond.

Perhaps something of the sensibility of Zen can become clearer by contrasting it to a Christian sensibility. Here is "The Eagle," a poem by Alfred Lord Tennyson:

He clasps the crag with crooked hands;
Close to the sun in lonely lands,
Ring'd with the azure world, he stands.

The wrinkled sea beneath him crawls;
He watches from his mountain walls,
And like a thunderbolt he falls.

This poem breathes power, muscle, substance, *thingishness*—the presence of being, not *being itself,* as is being indirectly represented by Bashō, but createdness. The eagle is in the solid world of mountain crags silhouetted against a real sky. And the eagle is personified; he is a *he,* not an *it*; he has *hands,* not claws. Even the sea takes on life; it *crawls.* Then when the action takes place, it does so suddenly and with a distinct sense that tragedy awaits its prey. In some ways it is a frightening poem. Nature is a wild thing, perhaps a bit like William Blake's tiger, "burning bright / in the forest of the night"—beautiful but dangerous.

Or consider this lyric by Emily Dickinson:

After great pain, a formal feeling comes—
The Nerves sit ceremonious, like Tombs—
The stiff Heart questions was it He that bore,
And Yesterday, or Centuries before?

The Feet, mechanical, go round—
Of Ground, or Air, or Ought—
A Wooden way
Regardless grown,
A quartz contentment like a stone—

This is the Hour of Lead—
Remembered if outlived,
As freezing persons, recollect the Snow—
First—Chill—then Stupor—then the letting go—[7]

If this poem is imbibed by a skilled reader (or even a reader who becomes skilled by slowly and carefully reading and rereading the poem), a whole world opens up. Dickinson is reflecting on the experience of the death of a dear friend, and she captures that experience in graveyard images and wonderment about whether there has been any atonement by Christ, any meaning to life, now or ever. Two short lines ("The stiff Heart questions was it He that bore, / And Yesterday, or Centuries before?") summon up in a good reader a large measure of the Christian worldview. Dickinson's *poetic intuition,* Jacques Maritain might say, pours forth in words that transmit her stunned skeptical reaction and its nearly nihilistic resolve.[8]

There is more than meets the eye or ear here. The poem evokes her inner struggles but also transcends her own experience and becomes an "objective correlative" for the almost universal experience of those whose worldview is primarily Christian. True, this worldview is not fleshed out as in Calvin's *Institutes* or Aquinas's *Summa Theologica*. But a piece of that worldview is embodied in a more powerful way than in any theological text.

The concrete terms—the images and what they suggest—give the poem its power. The *tombs,* the *feet mechanical* treading a *Wooden way* that disappears into nothingness, the *leaden hour,* the experience of *freezing*: these flesh out both the facts of death and its feeling.

Of course the poem has a linguistic structure; all poetry—good and bad—has that. For a poem to be good, however, it must have a structure worthy of its subject. This poem does. Its rhyme and near rhyme are conventional; its use of dash instead of traditional commas and periods violates traditional punctuation but succeeds because it suggests bursts of poetic intuition that when combined lead to the effect Dickinson wanted.

Finally, for a skilled reader the poem evokes an aesthetic experience, that is, a feeling that results from experiencing the Secondary World constructed by the writer.[9] One's feeling of agony at the death of King Lear, for example, is different from the similar feeling triggered by the death of a national figure such as John F. Kennedy or Princess Diana. Lear's death is not "real death" but "imitated death." It takes place on stage. The death of Dickinson's friend in "After great pain" takes a similar place on a page or in our imagination. Yet through Shakespeare's and Dickinson's poetic intuition and literary skill, our feeling itself is real.

Surely that feeling is deeper than, as Alexander Pope might say, "what oft was thought but ne'er so well expressed." The feeling is not just expressed; it is stimulated in the reader. Nor is the emotion maudlin or sentimental. We are more likely to say, "Ah, so it is," as we compare the world of the poem and the emotions it evokes with the events of our own lives and the emotions they evoke.

Longer poems, novels and dramas can, of course, convey a worldview that is both broader and more complex. With dramatic conflict expressed in both issues and characters, a wide range of ideas and emotions can play out on stage or in a fat novel. There is no gainsaying that Dostoyevsky's *The Brothers Karamazov* and *Crime and Punishment* are "greater" works of art than a sonnet, even one by Shakespeare. Their scope is almost as panoramic as life itself, and their depth is even greater than that of our own life, for here we see through eyes that see more than we do. The novelist's gift of poetic intuition grants him not only greater insight into human character but also greater ability to express that insight so that the reader begins to see some, if not all, the novelist sees. As Joseph Conrad said, "My task which I am trying to achieve is, by the power of the written word to make you hear, to make you feel—it is, before all, to make you see."[10]

Some novels embody their worldview primarily in characters or character development; others do so largely by action, still others by imagining the inner workings of a mind—that of the novelist or of one or more of his or her characters. And, of course, there are philosophical novels, like Camus's *The Plague* and Saul Bellow's *Mr. Sammler's Planet,* where ideas play a heavy role. Literature takes a multitude of forms, employs a multitude of techniques. What makes a text a piece of literature, however, is none of these. It is rather the effective and affective embodiment of a worldview (or piece of a worldview), written in such a way that it creates in the reader not only an intellectual understanding of the worldview but a sense of how it feels to hold that view. As Yvor Winters says, a literary work "should offer us new perceptions, not only of the exterior universe, but of human experience as well; it should add, in other words, to what we have seen."[11]

At one point in my developing understanding of literature, I wanted Joseph Conrad's view of the artist to be true. It squares with the Christian understanding of truth and reality. He wrote, "A work that aspires, however humbly, to the condition of art should carry its justification in every line. And art itself may be defined as a single-minded attempt to render the highest kind of justice to the visible universe, by bringing to light the truth, manifold and one, underlying its every aspect."[12] Conrad believed that there is not only a unified truth to the visible world but a unified truth to the invisible as well. But for a long time now, a century and a half perhaps, that notion of truth and reality no longer holds sway in the Western world. If Conrad's definition of art is correct, there has been very little of it in the twentieth century and even less as we begin a new millennium. Modern readers, Christians included, have to become satisfied with identifying worthy literature with those texts that help us *hear, feel* and *see* the world from the standpoint of the artist, the characters or both.

Take this short lyric by Stephen Crane:

A learned man came to me once.
He said, "I know the way,—come."
And I was overjoyed at this.
Together we hastened.
Soon, too soon, were we
Where my eyes were useless,
And I knew not the ways of my feet.
I clung to the hand of my friend;
But at last he cried: "I am lost."[13]

Here is the taste and feel of nihilism. The word is not used. No idea is directly stated, but an overwhelming dark sense of despair exudes from the poem. The world of this poem is bleak indeed, and we see/sense/understand it. Certainly I do, and I do it as a Christian. What makes this simple verse literature is its ability to impress on the reader the insight of the author and his or her view of the world, or a view of the world that the author wants the reader to feel and understand. Crane's poetry in general is one sustained cry of anguish. But it is a cry we all should hear, because not only is it Crane's cry, but it is, or should be, the cry of everyone who faces a world without the biblical God. The truth Crane's poetry contains, then, is not the truth of its worldview but the truth of the character and consequences of his worldview. If God is a villain, a trickster or an indifferent abstraction, then Crane's poem tells us something very important. There is no solace in such a world.

Is this, then, a Christian poem in spite of itself? No. Of course not. But it is a poem that gives Christians and everyone who pays attention a glimpse of the world after the death of God, as Nietzsche has described it, for example, in his parable of the Madman who sought God, couldn't find him and contemplated the consequences.[14]

In conclusion, then, what makes my definition of literature Christian is that it accounts for the power we feel from all great poetry whether written within a Christian worldview or not. It also acknowledges God's gift of poetic intuition to all great writers. All inspiration is rooted in God the Creator. And all truth is God's truth, is it not? Some of God's truth lies buried unless some artist exposes it. We have in Crane's nihilistic lyric a glimpse of the truth of nihilism—that nihilism ends in despair. In much of Dickinson's poetry we have the truth of the skeptic drawn to Christian faith but only at the edge of belief.[15] In Bashō's haiku we have the truth of the Zen sense of reality (not that the Zen view is true but that the poem reveals what that view actually is both in idea and in palpable sense). So great writers are great not because they convey the truth of reality itself but because they convey the sense and feel of reality as experienced within any of a wide variety of worldviews.

Emily Dickinson caught the subtlety of truth in poetry:

Tell all the Truth but tell it slant—
Success in Circuit lies
Too bright for our infirm Delight
The Truth's superb surprise
As Lightning to the Children eased
With explanation kind
The Truth must dazzle gradually
Or every man be blind—[16]

"The poet . . . thinks," Maritain says. "And poetic knowledge proceeds from the intellect in its most genuine and essential capacity as intellect through the indispensable instrumentality of feeling, feeling, feeling." Yet it is not emotion that is expressed. Poetry is not the "thrill in the poet which the poem will 'send down the spine' of the reader."[17] But feeling must be there. As Dickinson said: "If I read a book and it makes my whole body so cold no fire can ever warm me, I know *that* is poetry. If I feel physically as if the top of my head were taken off, I know *that* is poetry. These are the only ways I know it. Is there any other way?"[18]

Indeed, ideas characterizing the artist's worldview inspired by poetic intuition and broadcast in words that fire the imagination and transmit truth to the reader through feeling: this is literature.

ARTIST–WORK–WORLD–AUDIENCE

Jacques Maritain liked charts. So do I. Perhaps figure 4.1 will help as we pursue further the various relationships between the artist, the work, the world (reality as it actually is) and the audience.[19]

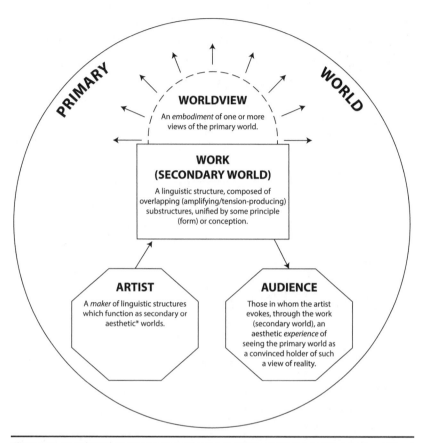

PRIMARY WORLD

WORLDVIEW

An *embodiment* of one or more views of the primary world.

WORK (SECONDARY WORLD)

A linguistic structure, composed of overlapping (amplifying/tension-producing) substructures, unified by some principle (form) or conception.

ARTIST

A *maker* of linguistic structures which function as secondary or aesthetic* worlds.

AUDIENCE

Those in whom the artist evokes, through the work (secondary world), an aesthetic *experience* of seeing the primary world as a convinced holder of such a view of reality.

Figure 4.1. *Aesthetic here means sympathetic but detached. What is being experienced is art, not life—we are seeing life, as it were, through the proscenium arch. In this way reality is embodied not as a philosophy but as an image or "imitation" defining the relation between art and life. The universal result of aesthetic appreciation is pleasure (one is first and foremost pleased by the fitting embodiment of life in art).

The work. At the center is the work itself—a Secondary World created by the artist from materials that exist in the world and the imagination of the artist (words, images, ideas, emotions).[20] It is a linguistic structure composed of overlapping (amplifying and tension-producing) substructures (plot, ideas, images, narrative action, rhythm, rhyme, various literary flourishes) sufficiently unified by some principle (form) or conception so that it hangs together. In any great literary work, whether lyric, novel or drama, there will be an overall singular conception that unifies all the diverse elements—the plot, the characters and their significance. If this unity is not present, the work will not be interesting enough to be readable.

When as an audience (or reader) we enter the Secondary World of a successful work, we will find among all the diverse elements something that pulls it all together, and even though that world may contain, as in science fiction or fantasy, elements of pure imagination, this unity makes it seem plausible. It can be a realistic world like that in a Steinbeck novel, a phenomenal world composed of the thoughts of characters as in a novel by Virginia Woolf, or even a fantasy world like Tolkien's Middle-earth. Middle-earth, in fact, is so vividly unified that for two hippie readers in the 1960s it became more real than the reality presented in academic history.[21]

The Secondary World of a lyric may be tiny. But simple as it is, it is *one* thing and not *another*. Take the Secondary World of "Jabberwocky," one of Lewis Carroll's most delightful nonsense poems:

'Twas brillig, and the slithy toves
    Did gyre and gimble in the wabe:
All mimsy were the borogoves,
    And the mome raths outgrabe.

"Beware the Jabberwock, my son!
    The jaws that bite, the claws that catch!
Beware the Jubjub bird, and shun
    The frumious Bandersnatch!"

He took his vorpal sword in hand:
    Long time the manxome foe he sought—
So rested he by the Tumtum tree,
    And stood a while in thought.

And, as in uffish thought he stood,
    The Jabberwock, with eyes of flame,
Came whiffling through the tulgey wood,
    And burbled as it came!

One, two! One, two! And through and through
    The vorpal blade went snicker-snack!
He left it dead, and with its head
    He went galumphing back.

"And hast thou slain the Jabberwock?

Come to my arms, my beamish boy!
O frabjous day! Callooh! Callay!"
He chortled in his joy.

'Twas brillig, and the slithy toves
Did gyre and gimble in the wabe:
All mimsy were the borogoves,
And the mome raths outgrabe.[22]

John Tenniel's original illustration for "Jabberwocky"

We don't need John Tenniel's illustration to see that the Secondary World in "Jabberwocky" is unified; the details are eccentric, but the world is believable on the level of both story and theme. Notice, for example, how many of the nonsense words have to do with the character of language and how it can be used to obfuscate and confuse and yet give a sense that the poem does in fact make sense. Most obvious is the combination of two words into one. *Slithy* is a portmanteau word, Humpty Dumpty explains to Alice; that is, there are two meanings in one word.[23] In this case, *lithe* and *slimy*. *Mimsy* combines *flimsy* and *miserable*.

Humpty Dumpty explains some words, however, in utterly whimsical ways. Lewis Carroll is, of course, having fun with language, but in this fun he is also revealing something about both human nature and the nature of language. He is telling the truth but telling it slant, suggesting, for example, that there are Jabberwocks among us—people who *jabber* when they *walk* and thus mostly talk nonsense, a nonsense that becomes sense to us anyway.

There is thus a connection between the Secondary World and the Primary World. The Secondary World imitates the Primary World. It tells the truth but tells it slant, and thereby reveals some of its nature that would not be revealed otherwise.

The world. What, then, is the Primary World? The Primary World is simply whatever reality actually is. Every waking moment we believe that we are perceiving the Primary World, but it is filtered to us through our worldview—those commitments and presuppositions that we take for truth without thinking much about it.[24] Or with a bit more precision:

> A worldview is a commitment, a fundamental orientation of the heart, that can be expressed as a story or in a set of presuppositions (assumptions which may be true, partially true or entirely false) which we hold (consciously or subconsciously, consistently or inconsistently) about the basic constitution of reality and provide the foundation on which we live and move and have our being.[25]

We live as if the world is actually the way we take it to be. Then sometimes we notice that reality does not conform to our worldview. Something doesn't fit. So normally we then change the part of our understanding that we've found to be in error. If we are serious about knowing the truth about things, we will constantly be improving the accuracy of what we believe.

So while the Primary World in its most general character never changes, our worldview may change a little or a lot.

In any case, both the Primary World and the Secondary World are understood by means of the worldview we believe best characterizes each one. In the literature already cited, several distinct worldviews are present. Bashō's "An ancient pond" is Zen in haiku form; Dickinson's "After great pain" embodies a skeptical version of a Christian worldview; Crane's "A learned man" expresses a form of nihilism. "Jabberwocky" presents a humorous take on a dangerous fantasy world in which young heroes can eliminate some of its dangers but still not change its basic dangerous character; something heroic happens, but nothing really changes. If this Secondary World is taken to represent our Primary World, then the poem reflects a modestly pessimistic naturalism.

Does the Secondary World identify the poet's own Primary World? Or must it be seen in light of its place in the story in which it appears? The answer is obvious. I'm tempted to say context is all. That's going too far. But I will say that the surrounding story—the whole text of *Through the Looking Glass*—must be examined, as must other literary work by the author. What worldview, then, is most likely to be the one reflected? This might be a good question for a student paper.

The artist. The artist is both a maker and a creator. On the one hand, the artist is a maker of linguistic structures, aesthetic realms made of words. At the same time, the artist is also a creator who by poetic intuition creates Secondary Worlds. In literature something new is brought into being. Artists are, of course, not creators ex nihilo. They create by making something new out of something already created. And what they create, then, has two sorts of relation to reality. A poem is an object like every other object in the Primary World. But, second, this object embodies and exhibits a Secondary World that did not exist before the poet created it. And this Secondary World acts as a giant metaphor or symbol or analogy for some aspects of the Primary World, both the immanent and the transcendent.[26]

The audience. As readers or viewers of art, we come last. Our task is to read or to perceive as well as we can what the artist has made. When the work does its work well and we are properly attentive, we often stand with open mouth, amazed at what is displayed before us, entranced by the Secondary World or the art of its construction. An aesthetic experience is invoked in us: we begin to experience what it would be like to view the world as if the Secondary World told the truth about the Primary World. Put in terms of the ancient critic Horace, the work has both delighted and taught us. Conrad says this:

> He [the artist] speaks to our capacity for delight and wonder, to the sense of mystery surrounding our lives; to our sense of pity, and beauty, and pain; to the latent feeling of fellowship with all creation—and to the subtle but invincible conviction of solidarity that knits together the loneliness of innumerable hearts, to the solidarity in dreams, in joy, in sorrow, in aspirations, in illusions, in hope, in fear, which binds men to each other, which binds together all humanity—the dead to the living and the living to the unborn.[27]

To do all of these things at the same time requires great art, great work from great artists. But it sometimes happens. Thank God, it happens.

WE ARE NOT ALONE

Literary art's sudden, startling truth and beauty make us feel, in the most solitary part of us, that we are not alone, and that there are meanings that cannot be bought, sold or traded, that do not decay and die. This socially and economically worthless experience is called transcendence, and you cannot assign a paper, or a grade, or an academic rank, on that.

—Lee Siegel, "Who Ruined the Humanities?" *Wall Street Journal,* July 13, 2013, pp. C1-2

THE ARTIST AND THE PRACTICE OF CREATIVITY

Again I want to proceed with the aid of a figure (see fig. 4.2).[28] It attempts to capture in a different way the relationships between the reader, the Secondary World, the artist and the Primary World (i.e., reality itself).[29] It is unashamedly and heavily dependent on Conrad.

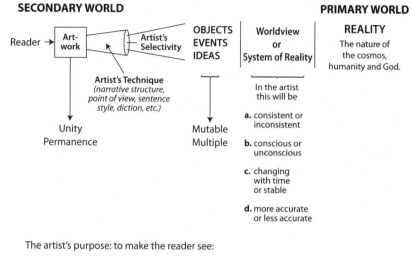

SECONDARY WORLD

Reader →

Art-work

Artist's Selectivity

Artist's Technique
(narrative structure, point of view, sentence style, diction, etc.)

Unity
Permanence

OBJECTS
EVENTS
IDEAS

Mutable
Multiple

PRIMARY WORLD

Worldview
or
System of Reality

REALITY
The nature of
the cosmos,
humanity and God.

In the artist
this will be

a. consistent or
inconsistent

b. conscious or
unconscious

c. changing
with time
or stable

d. more accurate
or less accurate

The artist's purpose: to make the reader see:

1. to picture in the mind's eye, to imagine;
2. to understand what happens and why;
3. to aesthetically experience the artwork or the Secondary World of the artwork;
4. to grasp the nature of the Primary World itself or as the artist has embodied it.

Figure 4.2. The roles of the artist, the reader, the Primary World and the Secondary World in the practice of creativity

At the far right side stands reality itself, the Primary World we all—artist, reader and literary work—inhabit. At the far left sits the reader with the work (book) in hand or the viewer with art object in sight. What is the connection between them? Primarily it is the artist.

The artist (let's say Joseph Conrad) understands the Primary World in accord with his worldview. He has the task of unveiling the nature of Primary Reality, a reality so mysterious that the reader (let's say my high school English teacher Lavonne Johnson) may not know it, in fact may not even know that she doesn't know.

She has, of course, both the Primary World and the Work available to her. She already knows something about the Primary World, but not all, certainly not all that Conrad can tell her through the work he has fashioned.

Conrad's task is to construct by artistic technique (narrative, image, point of view, sentence style, diction) an imaginary Secondary World that will stand on its own. He will do so by selecting objects, events and ideas that present his worldview, that is, his take on what reality actually is. The

Secondary World, in other words, is an interpretation. It imitates and interprets the Primary World by means of words that stand for more than they immediately signify.

WAKE UP

Why are we reading, if not in hope of beauty laid bare, life heightened and its deepest mystery probed? Can the writer isolate and vivify all in experience that most deeply engages our intellects and our hearts? Can the writer renew our hope for literary forms? Why are we reading if not in hope that the writer will magnify and dramatize our days, will illuminate and inspire us with wisdom, courage, and the possibility of meaningfulness, and will press upon our minds the deepest mysteries, so we may feel again their majesty and power? What do we ever know that is higher than that power which, from time to time, seizes our lives, and reveals us startlingly to ourselves as creatures set down here bewildered? Why does death so catch us by surprise, and why love? We still and always want waking. We should amass half dressed in long lines like tribesmen and shake gourds at each other, to wake up; instead we watch television and miss the show.

Annie Dillard, *The Writing Life* (New York: Harper Perennial, 1989), pp. 72-73

The reader's task is to grasp the nature of the Secondary World and see in it what the artist has understood the Primary World to be. As Conrad says, the artist is called to halt readers' attention to the ordinary tasks of the day and to cause them "to glance for a moment at the surrounding vision of form and color, of sunshine and shadows; to make them pause for a look, for a sigh, for a smile—such is the aim, difficult and evanescent, and reserved only for a few to achieve. . . . And when this is accomplished—behold!—all the truth of life is there: a moment of vision, a sigh, a smile—and the return to an eternal rest."[30]

There is, of course, in Conrad's description more than a hint of the romantic notion of the artist as a source of revelation that is as significant as the Bible. In adapting his language I want to assure readers that I have not replaced Jesus with Joseph. All that Conrad as artist can do is to reveal what he believes reality to be. He has no more authority than any of us who read his work. But most would agree that any great writer or artist has indeed seen something that few others have seen. We stand in need of his vision, even if it lacks the authority of God and his prophets.

In short, the artist's purpose is to make the reader *see*: (1) to imagine, to picture a Secondary World in the mind's eye, (2) to understand what happens in the Primary World and why, (3) to experience aesthetically the work and its Secondary World and (4) to thereby grasp the nature of reality as the artist has given it form.

THE SKILLED READER

The effect of any artwork is heavily dependent on the audience—reader, listener or viewer. What makes a skilled audience? Here I will focus on the reader.

First, skilled readers pay attention. Let's take poetry. I recall an assignment early in my college career. We were to read and be able to discuss the meaning of a poem by Keats. I was baffled until I looked up a few words in the dictionary. Suddenly—miracle of miracles—the poem opened up to me. How could I not have known this before? Well, better to learn late than not at all.

As readers we begin with the concrete and end with the general. If we are skilled, we will first be sure that we have absorbed the literary work itself. With lyric poetry, repeated reading is important, even readings in which we ignore the fact that we do not understand all the words. The goal is to have the poem sink deep into our consciousness, letting its verbal life direct our own. We want to react to the poem, not to what we prematurely determine the poem to be.[31]

Then we begin to pay attention to the details—the words we need to look up, the metaphors and their structure in the poem, the sound structures (rhyme, rhythm, onomatopoeia, for example), the metrical structure, the syntactical structure, the way the poem is laid out on the page.[32] Having grasped the details, eventually we will want to see the poem on its own as a whole.

At this point we should be able to say something about its worldview, though what we understand may be altered as we continue to reflect on the work in its broader social contexts.

Second, the skilled reader *interprets* the poem in the contexts of other similar and different poems, its place in intellectual and social history, and its connection to the life of the poet.

Finally, the skilled reader grasps the worldview of the poem and considers how it modifies his or her own grasp of reality or why some or all of its perspective must be rejected as an insight into the nature of the Primary World. In short, the skilled Christian reader brings to bear the Christian take on reality, consigns the literary work to its proper place as an artwork and as an embodiment of a view of reality and participates aesthetically in the worldview by sensing what it feels like to view reality from that point of view.

As C. S. Lewis says, the reader "need not approve of the Logos" (by which he means any truth claims the worldview involves).[33] Even when we do not endorse the worldview, though, as good readers we may well gain "an enlargement of our being."[34] Literature "admits us to experiences other than our own."[35] Lewis concludes *An Experiment in Criticism* with these eloquent words:

> In reading great literature I become a thousand men and yet remain myself. Like the night sky in the Greek poem, I see with a myriad of eyes, but it is still I who see. Here, as in worship, in love, in moral action, and in knowing, I transcend myself; and am never more myself than when I do.[36]

Thank you, Professor Lewis! I love to see with myriad eyes not my own. And what I see are signals of transcendence.

THE ARGUMENT FROM LITERARY THEORY

But how do these signals become an apologetic for the Christian faith? How do they trigger that impulse we have to see beyond this material world and find ourselves in the presence of God? We need some examples of "God adumbrations" in literature. We will find a few of them in the following chapter.

5

BRIGHT WINGS AND WOBBLING LIGHTHOUSES

An Argument from Gerard Manley Hopkins and Virginia Woolf

> ❭◆❬

The entire bay quivered; the lighthouse wobbled;
and she had the illusion that the mast of
Mr. Connor's little yacht was bending
like a wax candle in the sun.

VIRGINIA WOOLF, *JACOB'S ROOM*

BEFORE I BECAME A DOCTORAL STUDENT, I had never read *Paradise Lost*. Amazing, yes, but a result of a quickly achieved undergraduate major in English and an MA program that did not close the gaps in the flow of English literature. That gap was closed at the University of Missouri at least in part because I was soon to teach English literature from Beowulf to Virginia Woolf.

I remember my first exposure to Milton's epic. I leaned back in my chair at my desk in the large English instructor office and began to read,

Of Man's First Disobedience and the Fruit
Of that Forbidden Tree, whose mortal taste
Brought Death into the World, and all our woe,
With loss of *Eden*, till one greater Man
Restore us, and regain that blissful Seat,
Sing Heav'nly Muse . . .[1]

On and on I read, utterly rapt until, brought into ecstasy by the most magnificent poetry in the English language, I stood up and exploded to my colleagues seated at their nearby desks: "Wow! Milton's great!"

I'd had no idea what I'd been missing by my suddenly obvious lack of exposure to the greatest of the great. No, I couldn't imitate the style of Milton's stellar epic. My response was reduced to babble. My closest colleagues, a couple who were already good friends, just smiled. The great unwashed was getting a bath.

We read great literature—Homer, Dostoyevsky, Dante, Milton, Austen, Woolf—and we are lifted out of ourselves into another world—a Secondary World that sometimes moves us into that transcendent universe next door. Such literature then becomes not only an apologetic for the Christian faith but its expression as well.

How does this happen? My argument proceeds by analyzing the work of two authors—the poetry of Gerard Manley Hopkins and the novels of Virginia Woolf. We begin with Hopkins, but we do not end until we see how their works argue for a direct perception of God's existence that deepens our grasp of why any apologetic can be successful.

GERARD MANLEY HOPKINS

Gerard Manley Hopkins (1844–1889) was raised as an Anglican. When he was a student at Oxford, he came under the influence of the Anglo-Catholic Tractarian Movement, and in 1866 he followed John Henry Newman into the Catholic Church. In 1868 he became a Jesuit and in 1877 a priest, subsequently serving as a parish priest and then as a teacher. Throughout his life he read and studied and wrote poetry, but very little of it was published until 1918, almost thirty years after his death.

The story of Hopkins the man is fascinating but not a part of my present interest. My argument is from his poetry, not his biography. I will start with "God's Grandeur," one of Hopkins's most glorious, most loved and most frequently anthologized poems.

> The world is charged with the grandeur of God.
>   It will flame out, like shining from shook foil;
>   It gathers to a greatness, like the ooze of oil
> Crushed. Why do men then now not reck his rod?

Generations have trod, have trod, have trod;
  And all is seared with trade; bleared, smeared with toil;
  And wears man's smudge and shares man's smell: the soil
Is bare now, nor can foot feel, being shod.

And for all this, nature is never spent;
  There lives the dearest freshness deep down things;
And though the last lights off the black West went
  Oh, morning, at the brown brink eastward, springs—
Because the Holy Ghost over the bent
  World broods with warm breast and with ah! bright wings.[2]

"God's Grandeur" is, first of all, a poem written completely within the Christian worldview. Many of the major concepts of that worldview are presented in bold relief—God as Creator of a world that reveals his glory, the rebellion of human beings and their pollution of his glorious creation, and the restoration of the world through the work of the Holy Spirit. The poem, in fact, is a Christian takeoff on the central theme of Psalm 19: to wit, that the skies and the material world bristle with signals of transcendence. "The heavens are telling the glory of God," says the ancient poet. And Hopkins echoes: "The world is charged with the grandeur of God."

Then the poem's brilliant, flashing images point sacramentally to a realm beyond the material world. Material reality—the universe as a whole (lines 1-3a) and human beings in particular (lines 3b-9)—signals the existence of the biblical God. Even in its fallen and broken condition, the world is not left to itself but is being renewed by the Holy Spirit (lines 9-14).

The poet sets fallen human beings firmly in their place as rebels against God and, long before the green movement, as polluters of the earth. Nonetheless, the earth is not lost. It will be reborn not by human effort but by the Holy Spirit, who sustains it, mothers it and fosters its return to its rightful place in the kingdom of God.

This poem embodies Christian theology at a profound level and testifies to the truth of the Christian faith. This is the way it is, the poem literally says. And the artifice of the poem—its rhymes and images and sprung rhythm—reinforces the message. If we read this poem well, we will gain an aesthetic experience of what it would be like to believe that the world is like this. If we are Christians and good readers, our aesthetic experience will be difficult to distinguish from our spiritual experience. We will be tempted to exclaim, "Hallelujah!"—a temptation not to be resisted.

This poem, in other words, is more than literature as defined in the previous chapter. It is an icon. We look through it into the mystery of God himself. Not only is the world charged with the grandeur of God, but so is the poem. Taken as a whole, the poem actually states the thesis of the argument I will defend below: There is the poetry of Gerard Manley Hopkins; therefore there is a God.

"The Grandeur of God" is a glorious poem, a delight on every level. But not every Hopkins poem is lit so brightly. Take this sonnet, often referred to as one of the "terrible sonnets," not terrible as poems but terrible in content. Sometimes readers with minimal understanding of the Christian view of human nature think these poems indicate Hopkins's loss of faith. Quite the contrary: they represent the deep depression of a soul sensitive to its depravity and its own lack of saving power.

> I WAKE and feel the fell of dark, not day.
> What hours, O what black hours we have spent
> This night! what sights you, heart, saw! ways you went!
> And more must, in yet longer light's delay.
>
> With witness I speak this. But where I say
> Hours I mean years, mean life. And my lament
> Is cries countless, cries like dead letters sent
> To dearest him that lives alas! away.
>
> I am gall, I am heartburn. God's most deep decree
> Bitter would have me taste: my taste was me;
> Bones built in me, flesh filled, blood brimmed the curse.
>
> Selfyeast of spirit a dull dough sours. I see
> The lost are like this, and their scourge to be
> As I am mine, their sweating selves; but worse.[3]

The Christian worldview is displayed no less here than in "God's Grandeur." But in this sonnet the consequences of sin focus on the sinner rather than on the world that suffers for human sin. The final line is a crushing but keen insight into what hell must be like.

A tour through Hopkins's poetry enriches a reader with profound grasps of God, the universe and humankind. A couple of other Hopkins poems will be discussed in a later chapter. As a presentation of and witness to the Christian understanding of reality, his work all but screams the argument: There is the poetry of Gerard Manley Hopkins; therefore there is a God.

The case I am trying to make, however, is not primarily that Hopkins's poetry signals the existence of God because it manifests the Christian worldview. Rather, I am trying to show that the art of Hopkins's poetry, its very aesthetic value, points to the existence of God. His poetry, as poetry, is a signal of transcendence. The two are, of course, entangled with each other. The art is appropriate to the content; it helps us feel with Hopkins what it is like to perceive the world from a Christian point of view. But the art, the beauty of the poem itself, points to the existence of the transcendent.

Perhaps it would be better to turn this around and say that God reveals himself through the art of poetry as well as through the content of Hopkins's poetry. This places the proper emphasis on the priority of being over knowing. We know God first not because of our own epistemic equipment (our ability to know anything at all) but because God reaches out to us. He speaks. In Hopkins's language, he *charges* the world with his *grandeur*. It is because of that charge, that speaking without words (as Psalm 19:3-4 says), that we can hear and see him through the world, through poetry and the art of the artist.

Arguing from Hopkins's poetry to the existence of God has some obvious intrinsic merit. After all, Hopkins as a completely convinced Catholic believes in God and expresses a Christian worldview in his poetry. But what about Virginia Woolf, who has no place for God in her sense of reality?[4] Can we make the same case from the art of her novels?

Virginia Woolf

Virginia Woolf (1882–1941) was born into a literary family. Her father, Leslie Stephens, was an intellectual—a literary scholar, a biographer and something of a philosopher. She was raised as a "rational moralist whose duty was to seek and hold fast to the truth as they saw it."[5] Her husband, Leonard Woolf, was a writer and, along with Virginia, edited and published the avant-garde writers of their day. The Bloomsbury group, a bevy of artists, writers and intellectuals, circled around the Woolfs and provided Virginia with both friends and intellectual sparring partners. She began writing book reviews and critical essays early on, but her first novel, *The Voyage Out*, was not published until 1915. *Jacob's Room* (1922), however, is her first major novel. It and *To the Lighthouse* (1927) are my favorites.

Virginia Woolf battled with profound depression and mental instability most of her life, making several unsuccessful attempts at suicide. In 1941, after putting the finishing touches on her last novel, *Between the Acts,* she filled her pockets with stones and walked into the River Ouse. But as with Hopkins, I will not be concerned here with Woolf herself but with two of her novels, *Jacob's Room* and *The Years*.

Jacob's Room. In *Jacob's Room* we see Woolf's first use of the narrative technique of stream of consciousness in a novel. Here are the opening paragraphs:

> "So of course," wrote Betty Flanders, pressing her heels rather deeper in the sand, "there was nothing for it but to leave."
>
> Slowly welling from the point of her gold nib, pale blue ink dissolved the full stop; for there her pen stuck; her eyes fixed, and tears slowly filled them. The entire bay quivered; the lighthouse wobbled; and she had the illusion that the mast of Mr. Connor's little yacht was bending like a wax candle in the sun. She winked quickly. Accidents were awful things. She winked again. The mast was straight; the waves were regular; the lighthouse was upright; but the blot had spread. (p. 1)[6]

In these opening lines, the outlines of the world of the novel are visible but vague. We don't yet know that Betty Flanders will be a key player in the Secondary World of the novel, nor do we know exactly what kind of world it is.

As we read further, we soon see that it is a world delineated by impressions of sound and color. The *gold* nib and *blue* ink of Betty Flanders's pen are put in straight, objective language. This is the way things are; the world of the novel is like the world of our own experience. There are gold nibs on old (to us, eighty years later) pens.

But then we read that the lighthouse *wobbles* and the mast of the yacht *bends like a melting wax candle*, and we know that we are seeing through Betty Flanders's tear-filled eyes, then through those eyes cleared by blinking. The lighthouse wobbles; the lighthouse stands upright.

Jacob's Room is a literary impressionist painting with a living, moving, speaking, thinking, feeling cast of characters. Betty Flanders would be at home in Monet's *Grainstacks, End of Summer* or in Georges Seurat's *Sunday Afternoon on the Island of la Grand Jatte.* The sky in Woolf's *The Waves* could be Monet's *Morning on the Seine, near Giverny.* With the impressionists, impression is all; the surface is what you see, and the surface is what you get. So it is in *Jacob's Room.* "Tears made all the dahlias in her garden undulate in red waves and flashed the glass house in her eyes, and spangled the kitchen with bright knives" (p. 2).

As we read further, we place Betty Flanders on a beach; we learn that she has frustrating children around her but out of sight; we know she is writing a letter and sitting as the subject of a painting. We learn that she is widowed, attends church and walks on the moor.

Ever advancing our thoughts and imaginations, the text propels us on, page after page. More and more clearly we come to see the world of *Jacob's Room* as a world of surfaces beyond which the actual presence of any substance at all is dubious. All of reality is put at risk of impression. No impression, no reality. In the early pages of the novel, the young boy Jacob is playing on the beach, running from a large black rock on which he had climbed and from a red-faced man and woman he has seen lying on the sand. For a moment he becomes disoriented.

> A large black woman was sitting on the sand. He ran towards her.
> "Nanny! Nanny!" he cried, sobbing the words out on the crest of each gasping breath.
> The waves came round her. She was a rock. She was covered with the seaweed which pops when it is pressed. He was lost. (p. 4)

As Jacob runs, he suddenly spies a skull under a cliff, and he runs "farther and farther away" until he holds the skull in his arms. Betty Flanders, his mother, having lost sight of him, comes round the rock, "covering the whole space of the beach in a few seconds" (p. 5). Now we see the beach, space itself, measurable in exact yards and feet, but experienced quite differently by young boy and mature woman. In the world of *Jacob's Room,* experience is the reality.

Perhaps the most telling mark of the impressionist world of *Jacob's Room* is the way it is constituted by being lit. Nothing can exist without being perceived; nothing can be perceived without being lit. And lit it is, this world of Woolf's imagination, lit with all the glory of sun, lamp and candle. As Betty and her two sons, Jacob and Archer, head back to their seashore home for the summer, managed by Mrs. Pearce, the sun discloses the path to them:

> A pale yellow light shot across the purple sea; and shut. The lighthouse was lit. "Come along," said Betty Flanders. The sun blazed in their faces and gilded the great blackberries trembling out from the hedge which Archer tried to strip as they passed.
>
> "Don't lag, boys. You've got nothing to change into," said Betty, pulling them along, and looking with uneasy emotion at the earth displayed so luridly, with sudden sparks of light from greenhouses in gardens, with a sort of yellow and black mutability, against this blazing sunset, this astonishing agitation and vitality of colour. (p. 6)

The time suddenly shifts to later that evening, when again light displays the world: "The bareness of Mrs. Pearce's front room was fully displayed at ten o'clock at night when a powerful oil lamp stood on the middle of the table. The harsh light fell on the garden; cut straight across the lawn; lit up a child's bucket and a purple aster and reached the hedge" (p. 7).

We now see Mrs. Flanders sewing, "large reels of white cotton and her steel spectacles; her needle-case; her brown wool wound round an old postcard. . . . A daddy-long-legs shot from corner to corner and hit the lamp globe. The wind blew straight dashes of rain across the window, which flashed silver as they passed through the light. A single leaf tapped hurriedly, persistently, upon the glass. There was a hurricane out at sea" (p. 7).

Rain dashes (not drops) flashing silver in the light. A leaf tapping on the window pane. Motion and sound join sight to spark interpretation: "there was a hurricane out at sea." Impression, sensation, interpretation. *Is* there a hurricane out at sea? Or is it only in the thought of Betty Flanders? In *Jacob's Room* it is not the accuracy of the interpretation that counts; it is only the impression and its interpretation. The light in the seashore cottage shines through the window and lights up the garden.

> The light blazed out across the patch of grass; fell on the child's green bucket with the gold line round it, and upon the aster which trembled violently beside it. For the wind was tearing across the coast, hurling itself at the hills,

and leaping, in sudden gusts, on top of its own back. How it spread over the town in the hollow! How the lights seemed to wink and quiver in its fury, lights in the harbour, lights in the bedroom windows high up! And rolling dark waves before it, it raced over the Atlantic, jerking the stars above the ships this way and that. (pp. 8-9)

The insubstantial world is awash in motion, vibrating, trembling and subject to extinction at any time: "There was a click in the front sitting-room. Mr. Pearce had extinguished the lamp. The garden went out. It was but a dark patch" (p. 9).

The garden "went out" when the light in the house goes out. So in *Jacob's Room* the world, the universe itself, goes out when the light goes out. Othello in Shakespeare's play says it well as he contemplates snuffing out the life of his beloved Desdemona: "Put out the light, and then put out the light."[7]

More and more as the novel develops we see the utter insubstantiality of its world. Woolf focuses, for example, on students who enter the university chapel: "Look, as they pass into service, how airily the gowns blow out, as though nothing dense and corporeal were within" (p. 31).

The novel itself focuses on Mrs. Flanders's son Jacob, who tries endlessly to become a "man of substance" (p. 36) but over and over fails to do so. Even lit by the light of Cambridge, the substance is never realized. The light of Cambridge turns out to be the light of Julian the Apostate, the emperor who violently opposed the light of Christianity and promoted paganism (p. 48).

In *Jacob's Room* God is dead, and the light that shines through the stained-glass windows of King's College Chapel, the glorious music that is sung by its choir and student congregation, the organ music that reinforces faith are all a vestige, not just of a dimly remembered past but of a past deliberately rejected. The light is now solely the light of the physical sun and the atheistic professors of the classical literature of a pagan past, a paganism that has lost its luster as a living religion and exists only as a "mobile army of metaphors" redolent of meaning but absent of content.[8] It is a light that will penetrate the souls of its students, erasing from them the darkness of Christian faith.

This light does not bring joy. And no one really sees anyone other than themselves. "Nobody sees anyone as he is, let alone an elderly lady sitting opposite a strange young man in a railway carriage. They see a whole—they see all sorts of things—they see themselves" (p. 30).

Jacob remains a shadow throughout the novel. Even his shadow turns out not to be cast by Jacob (p. 136). More important, he dies offstage, between the end of the penultimate chapter and the beginning of the final one. Is it in Flanders, where the fighting in the Great War was so heavy, his name thus foreshadowing that he was doomed to die young without ever achieving a singular identity, let alone greatness? Has he all along been "driven by an unseizable force"? Perhaps so: "This, they say, is what we live by—this unseizable force" (p. 176).

A WILL O' THE WISP

[The] self was an elusive will o' wisp, always just ahead on the horizon, flickering and insubstantial, yet enduring. She believed the individual identity to be always in a flux, every moment changing its shape in response to the forces surrounding it: forces which were invisible emerge, others sink silently below the surface, and the past, on which the identity of the present moment rests, is never static, never fixed like a fly in amber, but as subject to alteration as the consciousness that recalls it.

—Jeanne Schulkind, introduction to Virginia Woolf, *Moments of Being,* ed. Jeanne Schulkind (New York: Harcourt Brace, 1985), p. 12

"What am I to do with these, Mr. Bonamy?" asks Mrs. Flanders of one of Jacob's still living friends in the final lines of the novel, as she holds out "a pair of Jacob's old shoes" (p. 201). Like the gowns of the Cambridge students, the empty shoes are never to be filled. In the world of *Jacob's Room* there is nothing to fill any shoes; there are only impressions, sensations and interpretations. But finally the latter run out. There are no more interpretations either.

Ontology is not the first thing most modern folk think about. Questions like "Who are you?" are rarely answered in an ontological fashion. Perhaps the most usual answer is simply "me." *I am me.* It's an existential answer; it says nothing about one's substance or lack thereof, whether one is merely material (matter and energy) or merely spiritual (a spark of the divine) or some mysterious combination of matter and spirit. But it says everything about the modern triumph of self-consciousness. "I am who I am" is neither said nor intended to be said as it was by the voice from the burning bush in Exodus. It is merely a declaration of our own self-conscious individualism: "I gotta be me."

How then does *Jacob's Room* argue for the existence of God? First is the very ability of Woolf to construct a Secondary World that is so unified, so consistently impressionistic, that it becomes believably real to readers. Her own ability to do this belies the view of the world she presents. She is, shall we say, the creator-god of this Secondary World. She must *be,* really *be,* or she could not create.

Second, she depicts characters who would like to escape their world. Their own psychological reality requires them to believe and to act as if there is something more than impressions, even though in *Jacob's Room* there is nothing more. The characters receive signals of transcendence that they do not pursue. For example, there once was a brilliant light in Cambridge, the light of the truth of the Christian faith. But this light is not recognized by anyone in the novel and is denied by Woolf, its creator. The signals of transcendence are simply ignored. We as readers, however, do not have to ignore them. They make sense out of the novel even if the novel itself denies that any sense can be made out of it.

But we must not miss a major value of the novel. In accordance with the definition of literature given above, *Jacob's Room* is "the embodiment of (1) a view of reality (2) captured in concrete terms and given (3) a linguistic structure which is appropriate to the various ideas and attitudes that make up the view of reality and which will evoke (4) an appropriate aesthetic experience in the skilled reader." Woolf has indeed shown us (and made us feel) what it would be like if the Primary World were like her Secondary World. It helps us see the utter despair that awaits an intelligent and reflective person who understands the Primary World as the world of *Jacob's Room.*

Traditional Christians, too, have something ironically substantial to learn from *Jacob's Room.* For as intent as they are on being biblical or orthodox, they often will reply to the question "Who are you?" with a relational rather than a substantial definition. "I am a sinner saved by grace" is a typical answer from a typically informed evangelical or fundamentalist. Rather proud to know that they are sinners, they forget that there is something prior to their status as sinners that makes them who they are. We are all first and foremost *creatures,* beings made by the One who really is the final I AM. Only after we say, "I am somebody," as Jesse Jackson gets children to say, can we say we are sinners. First comes our own being; then comes the relation of our being to all else. And what we are in relationship with depends on our fundamental nature as *created in the image of God.* Since we do indeed have a broken relationship to God and are not as we were intended to be, we are in fact sinners. But this is a secondary matter—vital to know, but secondary.

Ontology is a primary matter, whether we think so or not. And Virginia Woolf gets us to think about that. That she does not show us any alternative to the insubstantiality of the world is no reason not to thank her for the vividness with which she presents that insubstantial world, how well she creates it in us, or makes us reenact the insubstantial world as we read *Jacob's Room.*

Jacob's Room is set in a world in which God is dead, but its focus is on the emptiness of being more than the absence of a God who cares. It is a universe that in some sense exists as phenomena humanly perceived. Jacob's longing is for substance of any kind, and human substance (i.e., significance) in particular. He fails to find it before his ephemeral life is snuffed out in war.

The Years. *The Years* (1937) continues a form of the stream-of-consciousness narrative technique. I choose this novel for four reasons. First, it is a remarkable piece of writing. Second, it presents in concrete form a view of reality that in the short run may well be true to human experience but in the final analysis is false. Third, even in its failure to be true to reality, it gives more than a hint of what is really true. Fourth, it is somewhat more antitheological than *Jacob's Room.*

The Years, a long and gracefully written novel, ends with these words of beauty and hope:

> The sun had risen, and the sky above the houses wore an air of extraordinary beauty, simplicity and peace (p. 435).[9]

Beauty, simplicity, peace. So this sentence proclaims. But as the reader clearly knows, it is laced with irony—as deep as any in the entire, often ironic corpus of Woolf's work.

A party has brought together the major figures of the Pargiter family, whose saga Woolf has been tracing from 1880 to the present (about 1937). The party has not gone well. No one can say what they would like to say, no one quite means what they do say, those who have had epiphanies of self-understanding are being self-deceived, no one knows either themselves or others, nor do they have even the faintest grasp of any significance in their long lives. When the children of the caretaker are brought in and asked to brighten the party with children's joie de vivre, their words are unintelligible, their voices harsh, their accent hideous: "There was something horrible in the noise they made. It was so shrill, so discordant, and so meaningless. . . . The contrast between their faces and their voices was astonishing; it was impossible to find one word for the whole" (pp. 430-31).

There is a disturbing inevitability to the course of the story Woolf tells. Every character is trapped in his or her own skin, bound by a unique subjective awareness. They understand neither themselves nor each other.

Virginia Woolf is rarely easy to read. Without one's full attention, this story quickly disintegrates. I can imagine many readers do not get past the first few pages. But while her novels demand attention, they repay it manyfold, none more than *The Years*. Here Woolf, now a master portrayer of intricate human relationships, recounts events in the life of the Pargiter family over some sixty years, stringing together eleven chapters, each recounting the events of only one day.

The settings of these scenes are unrelentingly spare. She does not sketch the scene, identify the characters and then describe the details of the day. Rather, she records snippets of conversations, constructs streams of consciousness and alludes to past events and characters. The result is a meaning that is first obscure, only to become clear pages later, if then. Moreover, she creates and invades the minds of her cast of characters seemingly without pattern. I say "seemingly" because with lots of attention and thought, one sees a pattern emerge.

Woolf has described this narrative method rather well in her essay "Modern Fiction," written some years earlier. Reflect, she says, on the experience of an ordinary day:

The mind receives a myriad impressions—trivial, fantastic, evanescent, or engraved with the sharpness of steel. From all sides they come, an incessant shower of innumerable atoms; and as they fall, as they shape themselves into the life of Monday or Tuesday, the accent falls differently from of old; the moment of importance came not here but there; so that if a writer were a free man and not a slave, if he could write what he chose, not what he must, if he could base his work upon his own feeling and not upon convention, there would be no plot, no comedy, no tragedy, no love interest or catastrophe in the accepted style, and perhaps not a single button sewn on as the Bond Street tailors would have it. Life is not a series of gig lamps symmetrically arranged; but a luminous halo, a semi-transparent envelope surrounding us from the beginning of consciousness to the end.[10]

There is no implicit or obvious order to experience. It comes to us willy-nilly. We make of it what we will. So the novelist, if not bound by convention, would depict life. Woolf seems to set for herself just such a task: "Let us record the atoms as they fall upon the mind in the order in which they fall, let us trace the pattern, however disconnected and incoherent in appearance, which each sight or incident scores upon the consciousness."[11]

Late in her life she seems more bent on discovering, and in her novels depicting, the significant patterns of life.

Perhaps this is the strongest pleasure known to me. It is the rapture I get when in writing I seem to be discovering what belongs to what; making the scene come right; making a character come together. From this I reach what I might call a philosophy; at any rate it is a constant idea of mine; that behind the cotton wool is hidden a pattern; that we—I mean all human beings—are connected with this; that the whole world is a work of art; that we are parts of the work of art. *Hamlet* or a Beethoven quartet is the truth about this vast mass that we call a world. But there is no Shakespeare, there is no Beethoven; certainly and emphatically there is no god; we are the words; we are the music; we are the thing itself. And I see this when I have a shock.

This intuition of mine—it is so instinctive that it seems given to me, not made by me—has certainly given its scale to my life ever since I saw the flower in the bed by the front door at St. Ives.[12]

In the final analysis that pattern, while it does show an implicit order under the chaos of events and thoughts, ends up being as meaningless as chaos itself. Take the several epiphanies that occur throughout *The Years*. Early one morning, Kitty Malone, now Lady Lasswade, walks in the woods near her manor house somewhere north of London:

> Suddenly she saw the sky between two striped tree trunks extraordinarily blue. She came out on the top. The wind ceased; the country spread wide all round her. Her body seemed to shrink; her eyes to widen. She threw herself on the ground, and looked over the billowing land that went rising and falling, away and away, until somewhere far off it reached the sea. Uncultivated, un-inhabited, existing by itself, for itself, without towns or houses it looked from this height. Dark wedges of shadow, bright breadths of light lay side by side. Then, as she watched, light moved and dark moved; light and shadow went travelling over the hills and over the valleys. A deep murmur sang in her ears—the land itself, singing to itself, a chorus, alone. She lay there listening. She was happy, completely. Time had ceased. (pp. 277-78)

This is 1914. We never hear of this epiphany again. For Kitty the transient, ephemeral, ever-shifting world of impressions that had once seemed to manifest a profound unity returns to its daily character. Confusion returns. Meaning vanishes.

Eleanor Pargiter too has an epiphany. In the midst of the Great War, with bombs bursting in London, she sees a pepper-pot as a "dark moor," partly as a result of wine: "A little blur had come round the edges of things. It was the wine; it was the war. Things seem to have lost their skins; to be freed from some surface hardness; even the chair with gilt claws, at which she was looking, seemed porous; it seemed to radiate out some warmth, some glamour, as she looked at it" (p. 287).

Later, the feeling returns and intensifies: "She lay back in the chair. Everything seemed to become quiet and natural again. A feeling of great calm possessed her. It was as if another space of time had been issued to her, but robbed by the presence of death of something personal, she felt—she hesitated for a word—'immune'?" (pp. 293-94).

The destruction of war has missed her; she is, and will be, preserved from death. But, of course, only for a time. Nicholas, a mysterious alien figure in the novel, has envisioned a New World, and Eleanor is captivated: "When will this New World come? When shall we be free? When shall we live ad-venturously, wholly, not like cripples in a cave? He seemed to have released something in her; she felt not only a new space of time, but new powers, something unknown within her. . . . We shall be free, we shall be free, Eleanor thought" (p. 297).

She even contemplates Virginia Woolf's own sense of a pattern beneath the chaotic surface: "Does everything then come over again a little differently? she thought. If so, is there a pattern; a theme, recurring, like music; half remembered, half foreseen? . . . a gigantic pattern, momentarily perceptible? The thought gave her extreme pleasure: that there was a pattern. But who makes it? Who thinks it? Her mind slipped. She could not finish her thought" (p. 369).

Dangling conversations, dangling thoughts, course through *The Years*. Scenes begin in medias res and end there. Slices of life, literary critics call them—slices that, pared from their context, hang precipitously till the next slice, a segment preceded by a gap, appears. Eleanor cannot finish her thought partly because this is a dinner party and other guests impinge on thoughts and conversations, but finally because a thought like the one she has begun can never be completed.

Her niece Peggy, though, does not yet realize this. At the same party, she becomes bored, picks up a book and opens it at random and reads:

> *"La médiocrité de l'univers m'étonne et me révolte,"* she read. That was it. Precisely. She read on. *". . . la petitesse de toutes choses m'emplit de dégoût . . ."* She lifted her eyes. They were treading on her toes. *". . . la pauvreté des êtres humains m'antéantit."* She shut the book and put it back on the shelf.
>
> Precisely, she said. (p. 383)[13]

Set to thinking such dour thoughts, she is interrupted. Eleanor has suddenly burst forth with joy: "'I feel . . .' she stopped. She put her hand to her head; 'as if I'd been in another world! So happy!' she exclaimed" (p. 387).

"Tosh," says her brother-in-law René, accusing her of "always talking about another world." No, she replies, "I meant, happy in this world—happy with living people" (p. 387).

This sets the young Peggy to thinking again. How can people in this world be happy? "On every placard at every street was Death; or worse—tyranny; brutality; torture; the fall of civilization; the end of freedom" (p. 388). Peggy, the younger generation, the one in whom all peoples of all times place their confidence, despairs of thinking: "Why must I think? She did not want to think. She wished that there were blinds like those in railway carriages that came down over the light and hooded the mind. . . . Thinking was torment; why not give up thinking, and drift and dream? But the misery of the world, she thought, forces me to think. Or was that a pose?" (p. 388).

She cannot trust her thinking, even her thinking about thinking. Laughter around her makes her thought dangle. It is never completed: "she tried to think herself away into the darkness of the country. But it was impossible; they were laughing. She opened her eyes, exacerbated by their laughter" (p. 389).

The laughter, however, has a strange effect on her. It produces an epiphany: "It had relaxed her, enlarged her. She felt, or rather she saw, not a place, but a state of being, in which there was real laughter, real happiness, and this fractured world was whole; whole, vast, and free. But how could she say it?" (p. 390). Like all "oceanic experiences," senses of cosmic consciousness, the insight is incommunicable, hers alone. She tries to articulate it, but what comes out is an insult to her brother. The epiphany is belied. A few minutes later she realizes this: "Yes, it was over; it was destroyed, she felt. Directly something got together, it broke. She had a feeling of desolation" (p. 392).

She will have to start over. And so would Woolf in the novel. Peggy does so by turning to the thoughts of North, her brother who has spent the past few years as a farmer in Africa. North does not fit into the company of the dinner party; he has been away from England too long. Most of those he meets at the party are either foreign, as is Nicholas, or a generation ahead of him. As far as he is concerned, his relatives of the English upper-middle class fritter their lives away talking about money and politics. He would talk "about the past and poetry" (p. 409), but no one, not even his uncle Edward, Oxford Greek scholar, will join him.

As he watches the bubbles rise in his wine, he is left to his own ruminations. He does not want life with a pattern, but life "modeled on the jet (he was watching the bubbles rise), on the spring, of the hard leaping fountain" (p. 410), not a place in an orderly world of money and politics but a way "to make a new ripple in the human consciousness, be the bubble and the stream, the stream and the bubble—myself and the world together" (p. 410). This he thinks to himself and wants to say to others, but he falters. He can't speak out or even continue with his thoughts, for he questions himself:

"How can I . . . unless I know what's solid, what's true; in my life, in other people's lives?" (p. 410). But a few moments later he is feeling as if "he had been in the middle of a jungle; in the heart of darkness; cutting his way towards the light; but provided only with broken sentences, single words, with which to break through the brier bush of human bodies, human wills and voices, that bent over him, binding him, blinding him" (p. 411). A moment later, he is again optimistic, seeing "the fruit, the fountain that's in all of us" (p. 412), and a moment after that down in the dumps: "A block had formed in his forehead as if two thoughts had collided and had stopped the passage of the rest. His mind was a blank. He swayed the liquid from side to side. He was in the middle of a dark forest" (p. 413).

By now Woolf wants us to see that whether up or down, North is under the influence not of his own clear thought but of the bubbling wine. In any case, Woolf leaves him pondering the fear that separates all of us from one another and struggling with the knot in his forehead: "Thinking alone tied knots in the middle of the forehead; thinking alone bred pictures, foolish pictures" (p. 414).

Asked to speak the truth, a truth the younger generation—he and his sister Peggy—can tell, he flounders. He cannot do it. He feels "again the constriction of the knot in his forehead" (p. 423). He wants "someone, infinitely wise and good, to think for him," but there is no one (p. 424). All he can do is to blurt out what he has heard from one even younger than himself earlier in the evening: "To live differently . . . differently" (p. 424). Then as the bubbles cease and the wine goes flat, North is reduced to solitary thought: "Stillness and solitude, he thought to himself, silence and solitude . . . that's the only element in which the mind is free now" (p. 424, Woolf's ellipses).

With this North slips slowly, dreamily into unconsciousness: "And he was floating, and drifting, in a shallop, in a petal, down a river into silence, into solitude . . . which is the worst torture, the words came back to him as if a voice had spoken to them, that human beings can inflict" (p. 424).

Unrelenting, Woolf drives home the emptiness of the lives of her characters. They are interesting in their own right. As readers we come to feel for them, but we see in them a vast desert, a wasteland of triviality, not because they wish to be trivial but because they cannot help but be so and, in the case of the major characters, are aware of that fact. The coup de grâce is Woolf's picture of Eleanor's final epiphany.

At the end of a dinner party, Eleanor, like North, in a semidrunken, sleepy stupor, yearns for an escape from this life to a better one: "There must be another life, here and now, she repeated. This is too short, too broken. We know nothing, even about ourselves. We're only just beginning, she thought, to understand, here and there. . . . She felt that she wanted to enclose the present moment; to make it stay; to fill it fuller and fuller, with the past, the present and the future until it shone, whole, bright, deep with understanding" (p. 428).

But she cannot have what does not exist in the world of Virginia Woolf: "It's useless, she thought. . . . For her too there would be the endless night; the endless dark. She looked ahead of her as though she saw opening in front of her a very long dark tunnel. But thinking of the dark, something baffled her; in fact it was growing light. The blinds were white" (p. 428).

As the novel closes, the sun is rising. But the spiritual reality for Eleanor remains dark. In the final irony of what may be Woolf's most ironic novel, day dawns as spiritual night looms large.

This is the truly depressing aspect of *The Years.* So much effort to construct a unified novel with such seemingly disjointed parts, so much depth to the characters themselves, so much effort on the part of the reader. And withal so little to satisfy either the characters of the novel or the readers, or, shall we sadly say, the novelist herself. Not long after she finished writing *The Years,* she committed suicide, an act attempted unsuccessfully in the novel by Rose Pargiter.

How closely does art imitate life? Or is it the reverse—how closely does life imitate art? One thing is clear. Suicide is not an unreasonable response to despair arising from nihilism, and Woolf throughout most of her life was troubled by nihilism. She misread the signals that pointed in another direction. But in her novels—great works of literature—she has left us signals of transcendence that show her to be not only a great creator of Secondary Worlds in the image of the great Creator of the Primary World but a great human being made in the image of the great God.

I have not written these comments on *The Years* at one sitting. The first were drafted one night as, somewhat depressed on vacation in Hawaii, I couldn't sleep. Go figure! But most of it I wrote a day later. I was not so depressed then. How could I be? I had listened to North say that it is fear that separates us. He is right. But as a Christian, I know that there is no reason to be afraid of reading Virginia Woolf. I know that Woolf is not right about the absence of God. She is blind to the light of the Son. And it is being aware of the presence of the Son—not just as the pattern that orders the seeming chaos of the world, but as the One who by taking on the pain of the world is the answer to the pain in the world, not just as the source of life a long time ago but as the sustainer of life today, the One who is the true fountain, who alone knows just what kind of living differently would be a proper goal of life—that is what banishes depression and brings a reasonable hope to all of life.

In the heart of *The Years* we find signals of transcendence, "echoes of a voice" that whispers, "There's more to life, more to the world, than meets the ordinary eye and ear." In Hopkins's terms, "There lives the dearest freshness deep down things . . . / Because the Holy Ghost over the bent / World broods with warm breast and with ah! bright wings."

THE MUSIC OF JOHANN SEBASTIAN BACH

The argument I have been casting in this chapter supports and illustrates three conclusions: (1) literature written from a Christian standpoint is a direct witness to the truth of the Christian faith (Hopkins); (2) while literature whose worldview contradicts or does not directly support the Christian faith, it often gives testimony for Christian faith in spite of this (Lem and Woolf); and (3) literature itself, as a substructure reflecting the full creative power of God, points beyond itself to a transcendent realm (Lem, Hopkins, Woolf and other writers).

The first conclusion needs no further illustration. Hopkins's poetry certainly is a witness to Christian faith. And it is obvious that the same could be said for any literary work with a Christian worldview. Before the last half of the nineteenth century most English literature would fit. The second conclusion is amply illustrated by Woolf's two novels, though here the illustrations could be endlessly multiplied. The poetry of Stephen Crane discussed in the previous chapter is an example. So, of course, is Stanislaw Lem's story of Mymosh. This short story, short and simple as it is, displays (perhaps unintentionally) the incoherence of the notion of the autonomy of reason as understood within a framework of naturalism.

DEPTH UNDER THE SURFACE

It was charged against the Christian that he wanted to get rid of himself. Those that brought the charge urged him to transcend his unsatisfactory humanity. But isn't transcendence the same disorder? Isn't that also getting rid of the human being? Well, maybe man should get rid of himself. Of course. If he can. But also he has something in him which he feels it important to continue. Something that deserves to go on. It is something that has to go on, and we all know it. The spirit feels cheated, outraged, defiled, corrupted, fragmented, injured. Still it knows what it knows, and the knowledge cannot be gotten rid of. The spirit knows that its growth is the real aim of existence. So it seems to me. Besides, mankind cannot be something else. It cannot get rid of itself except by an act of universal self-destruction. But it is not even for us to vote Yea or Nay. And I have not stated my arguments, for I argue nothing. I have stated my thoughts. They were asked for, and I wanted to express them. The best, I have found, is to be disinterested. Not as misanthropes dissociate themselves, by judging, but by not judging. By willing as God wills.

During the war I had no belief, and I had always disliked the ways of the Orthodox [Jews]. I saw that God was not impressed by death. Hell was his indifference. But inability to explain is no ground for disbelief. Not as long as the sense of God persists. I could wish that it did not persist. The contradictions are so painful. No concern for justice? Nothing of pity? Is God only the gossip of the living? Then we watch these living speed like birds over the surface of a water, and one will dive or plunge but not come up again and never be seen any more. And in our turn we will never be seen again, once gone through that surface. But then we have no proof that there is no depth under the surface.

[Spoken by Mr. Sammler, a Jewish refugee from Poland, puzzled over his own existence, its relevance, value and meaning]

—Saul Bellow, *Mr. Sammler's Planet* (New York: Fawcett World Library, 1969, 1970), p. 215

The truth of the third conclusion is harder to confirm. I shall try to do so by going around the barn, as we might say in the Sandhills, or telling the truth by telling it slant, as Emily Dickinson might say.

Among their long list of arguments for the existence of God, Peter Kreeft and Ron Tacelli suggest the argument from aesthetic experience. Their statement of the argument is odd. In fact, I suspect that it is not an argument at all but rather an observation about how people arrive at some of their beliefs, especially those that involve human values or other persons. The "argument" is this:

- There is the music of Johann Sebastian Bach.

- Therefore there must be a God.

- You either see this or you don't.[14]

This "argument" seems to me to work solely by intuition. Either you see it or you don't.

Many Christian apologists pay little attention to intuition. Rather they give evidence and human reason the more major role. But I don't want to downplay the role of intuition. In fact I want to build on it. Some of the workings of the mind remain an utter mystery, even after they have been plumbed by philosophers and scientists. We do not know either how or why we see (that is, grasp the truth of) what we see. Knowledge itself is immediate. This is the case from *I am awake* to *Here is my brother,* from *The time is now 5 o'clock* to *My wife is faithful.*

I am not saying that there is no evidence for any of these pieces of knowledge. But whatever evidence there is, whatever reasoning deals with the evidence—inductive, deductive, abductive—our sense of the truthfulness of this knowledge is unanalyzable. Either we see it or we don't. Indeed, apologetics ends in the mystery of knowing; and knowing ends in the mystery of being.

In other words, who we are determines what we know. This, it seems to me, is what God says to Isaiah (Isaiah 6:10), and Jesus (Matthew 13:13-15) quotes it to his disciples:

And he said, "Go and say to this people:

'Keep listening, but do not comprehend;
keep looking, but do not understand.'

> Make the mind of this people dull,
>> and stop their ears,
>> and shut their eyes,
> so that they may not look with their eyes,
>> and listen with their ears
> and comprehend with their minds,
>> and turn and be healed." (Isaiah 6:9-10)

God was preparing his prophet for what would happen when he proclaimed the word of the Lord. Isaiah had, of course, already accepted and was obeying God's call. Isaiah would hear; his disciples who also obeyed God would hear; anyone who ceased rebelling and obeyed God would hear. And as that played out, what a Word it was—all sixty-six chapters of it!

Jesus was preparing the disciples for the same thing—the proclamation of Jesus, the very Word of God. If people were to understand the words of the prophets and the Word testified to by the disciples, they too would have to cease their rebellion. When Jesus spoke to them, they were already doing that. They were on their way. But many—perhaps most—of those to whom the disciples would go would not cease their rebellion; their ears would thus be stopped.[15]

Hearing and seeing means knowing and understanding. How that happens is a mystery. Only because we are images of God embedded in the reality of God and his world, and only because he enables our intellect to function as he has made it to function, can we know anything at all. We really do not, and I would add *cannot*, understand how it is we understand.

Of course, many people do understand at least something about God. They can intuit the existence of God. Calvin spoke of the *sensus divinitatis*—a faculty of the mind, a piece of our epistemic equipment, by which we directly perceive the existence of the divine.[16] People don't need to give any deep reason for their grasp of God's existence; their grasp is sure without it. Abraham Kuyper said that through the *sensus divinitatis* God "enters *into immediate fellowship with the creature*. . . . At every moment of our existence, our entire spiritual life rests in God himself."[17]

If intuitive believers are asked for reasons, they often say something like "Look around you. How did all this stuff [the psychological certitude of which is likewise intuited] get here? How did it get to be so complex? And so orderly? Can't you *see* that there must be a Creator-Designer of some kind?" Some of these reasons are abductive; they argue toward a *best* explanation. Some reasons can be stated in syllogisms. But both the formal arguments and the abductive reasoning are after the fact. People have sensed the existence of something that transcends ordinary reality, and these are reasons they come up with when asked. They have come to know before they can explain why they know. Theirs is an apologetic beyond reason. There is more to knowing than they and we will ever know.

EYES THAT SEE GOD

There is an inward power, or ability, or faculty in man which is deeper than the ordinary cognitive powers. That is why Scripture can speak of a hearing which does not hear, and a seeing which does not see. It is this inward power or ability which, when sound and whole, has *an intuitive power for recognizing God and his truth.* . . .

We are further driven to the conclusion that this spiritual perceptivity was part of the *imago Dei.* Levels of perception exist now among men. . . . The clever person sees the point of a barb, or the force of a satire, or the meaning of an illustration which eludes the ordinary person; the sensitive moral person sees the ethical issue in a situation which escapes the brutal man. The Scriptures also see man in depth. Man does have "eyes of the heart" and these "eyes of the heart" must have been clear and unclouded in the day of man's creation. There are eyes which see pictures and landscapes; there are eyes that see relationships among concepts and sentences—brilliant, logical, analytical eyes; there are eyes which see beauty; there are eyes which see the sublime in human experience or in nature; there are eyes which see the finer moral points of our common life; *and there are eyes that see God!*

—Bernard Ramm, *Witness of the Spirit* (Grand Rapids: Eerdmans, 1959), pp. 36-38

Kreeft and Tacelli's argument, if it is one, is similar. People sensitive to the aesthetic value of music hear Bach and immediately perceive something glorious. They may not identify this glory with the glory of God, but they can't imagine that glory being accounted for in material terms. That is, they perceive a quality not to be accounted for by any technical analysis of the sequence and rhythm of the notes. The music in its performance points to something transcendent. Those who know that Bach was a Christian and dedicated his music to the glory of God will have no difficulty in giving a more specific definition to the God they perceive behind the music. But all sensitive listeners will recognize that the music points beyond itself, beyond its material form, to something Other.

I am tempted here to borrow the language of Friedrich Schleiermacher and make of it something he would not. This is, I know, a scholarly sin, one that is committed, I'm afraid all too often. Still, hear Schleiermacher's description of religion and substitute *literature*: "Without being knowledge, it [literature, music and art] recognizes knowledge and science. In itself it is an affection, a revelation of the Infinite in the finite, God being seen in it and it in God."[18]

Schleiermacher is expressing, in his usual dialectic form, a conception of religion that is, or is very near to, pantheism. Forget that. In the sense I take it, literature does indeed reveal in nondialectic form the infinite God in the finite literary work—the Infinite in the finite, that is, the transcendent in the immanent.

When Kreeft and Tacelli say, "You either see this or you don't," they are (in my understanding) pointing to the immediacy of the perception—its sudden thereness. Such immediacy must be the case in any perception whatsoever, even the perception that any particular logical argument is valid. There is a mystery in perception itself.

I do not want to make too much of the specific terms of Kreeft and Tacelli's argument. But I do want to make something of its form. Let me restate it in more general terms:

> There are the phenomena of literature.
> Therefore there must be a God.
> Either you see this or you don't.

I believe that a case for the existence of God can be made from any piece of literature. First, literature itself shouts out: Human beings are significant. Their significance cannot be well explained by reference solely to the material world. One cannot derive *ought* from *is*, unless that which *is* is already a value. The "isness" of the material world does not contain a moral dimension: pure matter cannot itself be a foundation for either *good or evil*. Matter is neither evil nor good in itself. Yet literature abounds with moral judgments, those made by the characters in this literature and those of the novelist or poet.

In other words, literature testifies to a transcendent realm in which are embedded the foundational values of its Secondary World. This is the case whether the particular work has a Christian worldview or not. Bashō's frog haiku may on the surface attest to a universe whose meaning or essence is unintelligible, but the haiku itself does not show this. It shows that Bashō longs for a final meaning, a deliverance from the weight of a merely material world. His search for this meaning has led him to deny that there is such a meaning. It has led him to a satori in which his own self has been negated. His solution is not so much a solution as the denial of a solution and a stoical resignation that ends in oblivion. The denial itself attests to its own falsehood.

As we have seen, Virginia Woolf's novel *The Years* does the same thing. And *Jacob's Room* shows the inadequacy of a phenomenological approach to understanding the world. So in ways both positive and negative, literature is a signal of transcendence. Let us come alongside each other as we read widely in literature from all sorts of worldviews. And let us look, and let us see.

The next chapter takes a different but related tack. It's a story about the *signaling* effect of poems and artworks. We'll follow the signaling crisis in the life of Jean-Jacques LeRoi, who acquires ears to hear and eyes to see.

6

NIGHT THOUGHTS AND DAY DREAMS

An Argument from Francisco Goya

> ◆ <

The imagination abandoned by reason
generates improbable monsters; added to this,
it becomes mother to the arts and
the fount of every marvel.

FRANCISCO GOYA, LINE ADDED TO THE ETCHING
THE DREAM OF REASON PRODUCES MONSTERS

WHAT HAPPENS WHEN GOD gets the attention of a seemingly satisfied secularist? Read on.

"Night Thoughts and Day Dreams" tracks the signals of transcendence that lead the protagonist from his sensitivity to the arts—especially literature and painting—to the truth in Christ. It's an old plot line used by Christian writers from time immemorial. The hero, Jane or Jill, Franz or Jack, faces a crisis of meaning; he or she wanders about reaching out for clues to the significance of life, at least his or her own life. Almost accidentally, Jill, say, finds a path (or rather, God finds the path for her); eventually she sees the truth and commits herself to it.

What can make this well-worn plot more than a cliché is that sometimes it attains the status of an archetype—a pattern deeply embedded in human nature. The story that follows illustrates how signals of transcendence from the arts can provide the impetus for a search that begins in sadness and ends in glory.

Many of the details are based on my own experience with art and literature. The main difference is that my commitment to Christ began before I had read much literature or seen any great painting of any great artist. Such paintings I did eventually see, first at the University of Nebraska, then in countless museums and art galleries around the world. I have, in fact, seen all the paintings mentioned in the story, which begins now.

NIGHT THOUGHTS AND DAY DREAMS

Jean-Jacques LeRoi, known to his friends as Jake, has been an English teacher at Kenton College in Ohio for twenty years. He has become a full professor and has served his turn as department chair. If you paid attention to the title of his doctoral dissertation, you would think his specialty was John Milton, but Kenton is a classical undergraduate liberal arts college where the liberal arts really reign. There are courses in business and accounting, prenursing and premedicine, and even computer science, but there are more majors in English and history, philosophy and fine arts than in any of the more career-oriented subjects.

Jake had thought he would one day teach his specialty to graduate students, but soon after he joined the faculty with his new doctorate, his interests broadened. Though he often bemoans the composition courses he has had to teach to the great unwashed first-year students, he has never regretted having to prepare lectures beyond his graduate school focus on the Renaissance and seventeenth-century literature. In fact, he has forgotten his intention to write scholarly books on Milton. Instead for his classes he reads and immensely enjoys the Great Books from Homer to Joyce and the whole corpus of English literature from Beowulf to Virginia Woolf and beyond. Emily Dickinson is now as important to him as John Donne, Walt Whitman as Edmund Spenser, Jack Kerouac as Sir Phillip Sidney. And when he curls up with a book in the evening, it is just as likely to be by Stanislaw Lem as by Charles Dickens.

Nor does he regret teaching bright undergraduates rather than average graduate students living in fear of their comprehensive exams. With the broader focus of his twenty years of teaching, Jake, now fifty, is in the prime of his career. Moreover, he is in the prime of health and, though paid only modestly, financially secure. He has never been seriously tempted by the nubile bodies of his students; his marriage is not only intact but flourishing.

Then in December, six months before the action begins, his wife contracts cancer. She dies in June. We pick up the story there.

Jake was stunned. He was completely unprepared. Mary's death was unthinkable, as unreal as an invasion from Mars. Yet there it was. He stumbled through the funeral and the burial, helped by his colleagues and favorite students. Then for four days he crashed. No one saw him. No one knew where he was. Then he appeared in his office back on campus, telling the dean that he would not be teaching in summer school and might not be back in the fall. "I am heading to Europe," he said; "I don't know where or how long I will be gone, but I will begin in England."

Still barely able to function, Jake found himself on British Airways 102. In his flight bag was a small anthology of poetry. He had wanted to travel light; he knew the bookstores in London and Oxford outshone any in Ohio, but he wanted some connection to the past. His plane landed in the morning, and Jake went to the small hotel where his agent had gotten him a reservation. He slept till early evening, had a simple meal in the hotel and began to walk the streets.

By this time Jake's mind was racing—dull, passionless, drained of feeling, but racing. He thought of Emily Dickinson: *After great pain a formal feeling comes,* he remembered. *The nerves sit ceremonious like tombs.* He shuddered. Exactly, he thought. Exactly. His mind was racing, his nerves dull. At seven o'clock on a drab June evening, Jake walked the streets past Parliament, Westminster Abbey, down the walks along the Thames.

Every line of Dickinson's poem he knew; every word was etched on mental parchment. It was the most beautiful poem he had ever read or taught. But it was literature then. *A formal feeling comes.* Yes, he thought, there it was: a stiff, distant, detachment of mind from body, emotion from mind, sensation from emotion. He was living the line. This wasn't literature. It was life.

He walked on and on. The ornate Thames Bridge he remembered not just from previous trips but from the ubiquitous pictures of London in tourist brochures and BBC television programs. Downstream along the river he walked, mind moving in dull circuits, repeating over and over again the lines from Dickinson. *After great pain a formal feeling comes. The Nerves sit ceremonious like Tombs. . . . This is the Hour of Lead . . . of lead . . . of lead.* He yearned for the final line: *First—Chill—then Stupor—then the letting go.* There had been the chill and the stupor, but no letting go.

In the days to come Jake continued to contemplate Dickinson's poem. He pondered Dickinson's sidelong allusion to the death of Christ: *was it He that bore, / And Yesterday, or Centuries before?* Was there atonement? Mary would have said so. She was, as he often told his friends, a card-carrying member of St. Andrews Episcopal Church. She attended. She served. She believed. She worshiped. He did none of these. But was she tuned into life as it really is? He didn't think so.

The next day Jake wandered into an art gallery that was not on any list of not-to-be-missed London tourist sites. Most of the paintings were undistinguished. But two were different. Serendipity—surely this was a stellar example. He was searching for nothing he could name—relief from grief, a period of peace to restore his material soul, something that would make him *let go.* What he found were slightly curious works of art, perhaps worth the huge prices listed on the walls, but not worth it to him. Then there were the two paintings very different from each other; these two, so the labels read, were not for sale but on loan from Sheldon Memorial Art Gallery at the University of Nebraska.

One, *The Man* by Ben Shahn, was in the style of social realism.[1] Against a dark gray background there emerged the outline of single human face, stark in empty loneliness and despair. Jake sat on a viewing bench, transfixed. He was looking in a mirror. The image was his. He didn't move; he didn't look elsewhere. He just stared. Others came by, glanced at the painting and moved on.

Jake felt he had to get away. He left the gallery, had lunch and returned. But afraid to encounter *The Man,* he entered the only other room. Again most of the paintings were not worth a glance, he thought. Some were—the only word he could think of—*gross,* twisted lines of a twisted mind, obsessed with Freudian sexuality and vague suggestions of perversion. He hated them and was about to leave. Then, alone and on a stand set five feet from the wall, was *Orange Abstract,* lit from above and glowing.[2] Again he stood transfixed. There were no images, no distinct lines, only thick globs of heavy oil paint, shaded from light yellow to bright orange. If there was an intended pattern, it was not apparent, not even after long contemplation. The painting's fascination lay in both the obscurity of its meaning and the brilliance of its color. Did it mean anything at all? Perhaps not. Then what accounted for his fascination?

The painting, filled with light, glowed. It reminded him of Gustave Caillebotte's *Paris Street; Rainy Day.* He'd seen that in the Art Institute of Chicago. Of course, Caillebotte was an impressionist; that artwork showed people, umbrellas, buildings and the glowing streets. *Orange Abstract* had none of these—only the radiance of the thick, variegated orange and yellow paint.

Jake made another circuit of the room; again he found nothing worth pondering. When he was about to exit, he turned for one last look. *Orange Abstract* seemed to be on fire. For the third time that day he again stood transfixed, this time because he had had a minor epiphany—an *aha!* re-action, a sudden *that's-it* insight. He saw now. The painting was simply itself. Abstract art was like that. On the one hand, *Orange Abstract* was itself its own meaning, ontological, more being there than meaning something. More than met the eye, but nothing ending in any thought. Like *The Man,* its image would soon become a permanent fixture of his subconscious, emerging at odd moments as he walked the streets of Europe, sought sleep at night and thought about his great loss.

After a few days in London, Jake traveled the Hardy country southwest of London and visited Thomas Hardy's grave in the tiny Stinson churchyard, finding that while Hardy's body lay there, his heart was buried in Westminster Abbey. He made a note to search there for the crypt. The rugged heath on the timeless hills took him back to *Tess of the d'Urbervilles* and *Return of the Native,* two of the novels he most liked to introduce to his American students. On his way to the Lake District, he stopped at Stonehenge and at Salisbury Cathedral, the site of William Golding's *The Spire* and Susan Howatch's Starbridge Cathedral novels. The weight of the historic spire had, as all tourists and readers of *The Spire* know, bowed the four columns holding it up, becoming a symbol for the overweening pride of the bishop and the builder.

Stonehenge was a puzzle of prehistory. The cathedral's history was just that, of no more significance to Jake than the ancient worship place of, so it was popularly thought, the druids. It was always a delight to see these places he'd taught about but had seen too little of. It increased his aesthetic enjoyment of the literature, but it did little for his spirit.

His trip north to the Lake District was slowed by heavy traffic and an accident. He pulled off the M6 and relaxed at a roadside pub with a pint. There they were again, that *Orange Abstract* and *The Man*: the one mirrored his mind, the other lifted him out of it. And then he *saw*. He knew.

Orange Abstract had hit him the same way as the tiny Zen rock garden he had seen in Tokyo when on R&R from Korea. It was years ago, when he'd served in the army for sixteen months after college. He had casually strolled near the Ginza in central Tokyo. Tall buildings towered above him. If it weren't for the Japanese language signs and the pachinko parlors, he could have been in Chicago. He stopped by a small rock garden, hidden from the street by a low wall. It couldn't have been more than five or six feet long and three or four feet wide. He was fascinated by its simplicity—some sort of gravel raked in furrows, with a half-dozen ordinary rocks of different sizes placed in no pattern that he could discern. He puzzled and he looked.

This plot of sand and rock, small as it was, filled his vision. Suddenly he was looking at a huge garden. Time was suspended; space had been transcended. It was no more than a moment. But as he thought about it later, it was if he had had a special insight, maybe an epiphany, a visit from the ancient world of traditional Japan. A few days later he came across a book on Zen Buddhism, illustrated with Japanese haiku, reproductions of Zen paintings and photos of Zen Buddhist rock gardens. Without the rigorous practice of Zen meditation, he opined, he'd had a taste of—what did they call it?—satori, an experience of "suchness," a realization that this moment of nowhere/no-when was a grasp of the really real which was somehow beyond the real, to be spoken of, if at all, in negatives—not this, not that. The experience didn't last long, but it had stuck with him for twenty-five years. With *Orange Abstract* that lone epiphany had been repeated.

In the Lake District he stopped in Grasmere, location of Dove Cottage, Wordsworth's home, had a pub lunch, ate some raw fish and suffered for it a few hours later. But not before he saw what he had come for—the inspiration for the paintings of Constable and Turner. He was sure that he would find that both artists had romanticized the vast scenes of misty clouds with shafts of sunlight thrusting through. He couldn't have been more deluded. Constable and Turner were realists. That afternoon in the Lake District he saw the paintings in the raw, untouched by subtle artistic brushstrokes. A light fog shifted slightly in a light breeze, and shafts of sunlight made the tree-scaped mountains glow. The Lake District was indeed just as Constable and Turner had limned it.

In London again, he visited the Tate, looking for more Constables and Turners. He found a few, but they were mostly seascapes and tall ships tossed by the waves but holding course. Then came another moment of illumination. Over a doorway to a closed-off room was the label "William Blake." He didn't know he would be seeing Blake's original etches and paintings—strange, sometimes bizarre graphic renderings of the angelic beings that haunted the poet's Swedenborgian imagination. Jake loved to teach Blake's *Songs of Innocence* and especially his *Songs of Experience.* Here too were the originals of Blake's illustrations.

Tyger! Tyger! burning bright
In the forests of the night;
What immortal hand or eye,
Could frame thy fearful symmetry?

In the printed reproductions of Blake's illustration, the flaming tiger had seemed something of a pussycat. Here the tiger leaped from the page. Who, indeed, dare frame its fearful symmetry? Only Blake.

What was it that came through to him from Blake or the painter of *Orange Abstract*? Why did the aura of Ben Shahn's *The Man* keep bubbling into consciousness? Something was happening to him that he found both frightening and immensely intriguing. What was it?

During Jake's journeys around England, he dipped into his anthology of poetry. He could not read far or dip deeply before he came on poems that both kept the wound of his grief from closing and acted as a balm on the open sore. Dylan Thomas's "Do not go gentle into that good night," he read; rather, "Rage, rage against the dying of the light" and "And death shall have no dominion." The former gave vent to his anger; the latter was no comfort at all.

He had seen his wife suddenly ill, then slowly dying. Bone cancer was the worst kind, he had been told. He had hoped nothing could be worse than this. And he hoped for its end as well. Mary suffered and he suffered with her. She had been a wonderful wife, bright but humble, a great cook, a great companion.

BLAKE'S FLAMING TYGER

Tyger! Tyger! burning bright
In the forests of the night,
What immortal hand or eye
Could frame thy fearful symmetry?

In what distant deeps or skies
Burnt the fire of thine eyes?
On what wings dare he aspire?
What the hand, dare seize the fire?

And what shoulder, & what art,
Could twist the sinews of thy heart?
And when thy heart began to beat,
What dread hand? & what dread feet?

What the hammer? what the chain?
In what furnace was thy brain?
What the anvil? what dread grasp
Dare its deadly terrors clasp?

When the stars threw down their spears,
And water'd heaven with their tears,
Did he smile his work to see?
Did he who made the Lamb make thee?

Tyger! Tyger! burning bright
In the forests of the night,
What immortal hand or eye
Dare frame thy fearful symmetry?

William Blake, "The Tyger"

She held a master's degree in genetics, had done research with a major geneticist and had her name on several scholarly articles. When they had children, however, she quit her job as practicing scientist to teach only occasional labs in biology at Kenton. Mary was a bit of a writer too, contributing articles on spiritual development to the *Episcopal Life* magazine. Their marriage, so unlike those in *Who's Afraid of Virginia Woolf?* performed by the college players a few weeks before her death, was a model for countless students who, through the years, married their college loves. Did they all work out that way? Probably not, but these students saw at least one example of how good a marriage could be.

"Do not go gentle into that good night" fit well with his own anger in the weeks before Mary's death. Mary too took up the theme, though not in anger, as she refused to give in to depression. At least at first. Then, as the disease progressed and pain medication was no longer effective, her resolve softened and she came to see death as a release. So did he. And she, for Christian reasons, could say with Thomas, *And death shall have no dominion.* But Jake could not. Nor did Thomas's pantheism give Jake consolation. He could never see Mary as *one / With the man in the wind and the west moon.* Dead is dead. The wound of grief remained open.

Meanwhile, his journey continued through literary England; the ancient castle ruins of Tintagle in Cornwall took him back to the days of King Arthur and those of Alfred Lord Tennyson. In Scotland he was buoyed up by Robert Burns. Across the Irish channel there was Trinity College, the *Book of Kells* and the poetry of William Butler Yeats. Boredom was not an issue. The more he traveled, the more he read, and the more he began to absorb the ethos of the British Isles, the stark hills of Staffin on the Isle of Skye, the craggy tors of Cornwall, the hills and dales of Yorkshire.

It was good for him to take this trip; gradually he brooded less on his loss and reflected more on the beauty of the Emerald Isle, the rugged terrain of Scotland and the crashing waves on the southwest coast of Wales. Even the cathedrals of England—Litchfield, Lincoln, Salisbury, Westminster—which he toured just to say he'd seen them, began a strange work in him. There was something about the stunning beauty of the Gothic architecture, the stained-glass windows, the murals of biblical scenes and especially the towering spires that pointed to something beyond themselves. But then the crucifixes and bloody images of Christ on the cross would disturb him. Why the cross, the bloody body, the excruciating pain of the crucified? For Jake even the resurrection did not make up for this. He could not get away from Dickinson's thoughts of death. *And Yesterday, or Centuries before?*

Jake decided to leave England for Spain. He'd been on the Continent but never in Spain. A quick flight to Madrid and a downtown hotel brought him into a different culture. The middling to poor British food and wine were replaced by excellent and inexpensive cuisine and red table wine that went down smoothly. There was also a lightness of spirit on the streets. And, of course, there was El Prado, the justly famous art gallery filled with bold works of the Spanish artists, chief among them Diego Velázquez and Francisco Goya. Major works by Pablo Picasso and Salvador Dali were in other, more modern museums.

The glory came with Velázquez. Jake was struck by his two huge paintings of an elegantly dressed young boy astride magnificent steeds, *Baltasar Carlos on Horseback* and *Baltasar in the Riding School.* He could imagine no other artist who could have captured in a single horse the *form* of horse, as a Neoplatonist might say. Velázquez did this with each of three horses, if one includes *Philip IV on Horseback.* Of course there were profoundly sensitive religious paintings as well. *Christ on the Cross,* for example, portrayed a sad but dignified Christ, not writhing in agony but at peace with his fate. Jake thought that Velázquez was depicting Jesus just after he spoke his last words from the cross: "Into your hands I commend my spirit." Jake was moved, not to worship but to honor and respect.

On the main floor there were also major works of Goya from all periods of his artistic life—agonized religious paintings such as *The Crucified Christ,* playful paintings like *The Straw Man* (four women tossing on a blanket a life-size straw manikin all akimbo), and two huge and famous paintings of the war with Napoleon, *The Second of May, 1808* and *The Third of May, 1808.*[3] Jake was immensely impressed with their art and grandeur, though the memory of none of them would stick past a few days.

Then he descended to the ground floor. In a far corner was a room of Goya's paintings. Set apart from the rest, they screamed out the darkness of Goya's mind. Terrible and terrifying—there was no other way to describe them. None of them was very large, but each one struck Jake with—he had a hard time describing it. *Macabre* did not do them justice. That would trivialize their effect. Rather, they struck him with a powerful and palpable sense of evil. No, more than evil, of deviltry, deliberate evil, as if a demon haunted the room seeking whom he might devour. No wonder the room's contents were isolated. No wonder no one else walked in while he was there.

Three of these "black paintings" were especially damnable—*Saturn Devouring His Son, The Pilgrimage of St. Isadore* and *The Witches' Sabbath.* Goya had several severe bouts with depression, the first in the 1790s when he lost his hearing, the second in the early 1820s. These three paintings, mostly in shades of brown and black, were from this second period of personal blackness. In *Saturn Devouring His Son,* a mad male figure chews on a tiny naked man. Saturn has already bitten off his head and right arm and is beginning to devour the left arm. Blood streams from the body.

In *The Witches' Sabbath* Satan as a goat sits with his back to the viewer and harangues the gathered coven. The pilgrim faces of young and old are ugly, twisted and redolent of evil. In the foreground is a nunlike figure who also faces the witches; to her left are bottles of potions. At the far right is a young woman with an undistorted face, seemingly mesmerized by the wickedness of the scene.[4] Unqualified evil pours from every brushstroke.

But for Jake it was *The Pilgrimage of St. Isadore* that over the next few weeks was to sink most deeply into and below his conscious mind. Here a band of pilgrims heads toward a Christian shrine. There could be no greater contrast to Chaucer's *Canterbury Tales,* where the pilgrims are a jolly band of men and women from a variety of walks of life, both secular and religious. Hope springs from every line of Chaucer's poem. Jake loved to teach Chaucer's tales; students actually read them instead of squeaking by on Cliff Notes. But in Goya's painting every pilgrim is in the agonies of wrenching despair. This is not a pilgrimage to a shrine of Christian hope; it is a pilgrimage to hell on earth.

Jake's visit to El Prado was devastating. Not since the funeral of his wife had he felt so utterly alone, so absolutely abandoned, so sunk in self-mortification and despair. Jake recalled a Goya etching he had seen elsewhere in El Prado. It was titled *The Dream of Reason Produces Monsters.* To this etching Goya added, "The imagination abandoned by reason generates improbable monsters"; and further, "it becomes mother to the arts and the fount of every marvel." The etching depicts the artist asleep at his desk and surrounded by swooping bats and owls, symbols not of wisdom but of stupidity. Surely this is Goya's premonition of his black paintings. Enlightenment reason had abandoned him.

In the following days Jake visited galleries with the work of Dali and Picasso.

Some paintings he found interesting, some both technically astonishing and obscene, but none of them replaced in his active imagination Goya's demonic images and the black despair they conjured up. It was time to move on to Salamanca, where the architecture of the ancient university and the storks nesting on the tops of chimneys acted as a balm to his soul. Then on to Barcelona, a city of light. His hotel was near enough to the great fountain where every evening music and lights played with the ever-changing spray of water. In the Picasso museum the collection of his early work proved for all time, in case anyone would doubt it, that the frequent distorter of the human figure could really draw.

Now restlessness took over. Jake had not, perhaps could not, come to terms with the death of Mary. He was reading lots of "great" poetry from his anthology. But the best it could do was stimulate his aesthetic sense and offer him the palliative of stoic resignation. The worst it could do, and that was more frequent, was to send him into a profound depression. Why did he read Sylvia Plath's "Lady Lazarus," with its macabre reflection on her three previous attempts to commit suicide? *Dying is an art,* she wrote, an art she does *exceptionally well.* Then, like Lazarus, Plath returned for a while to ordinary life. One day another of Plath's attempts was successful. Where is Lady Lazarus now? Mary, where are you now?

The poetry of Jake's own academic specialty was no better. The metaphysical confidence of John Donne's "Death be not proud" was too stern and abstract. The softer strains of George Herbert were too pious. Milton spoke of a *fortunate fall*; it was good that Adam and Eve rebelled because it provided a way for God to show the depth of his love for his creation. That was too paradoxical for his rational mind to swallow. He could not bridge the metaphysical gap between his own Enlightenment deism and the foundation on which these poets based their hope. Certainly he would not descend to Plath's nihilism, but neither could he accept the Christian hope.

His experience in poetry paralleled his experience of painting. The glowing images of the resurrected Jesus were fantastic; the crucifixion scenes gruesome; the soaring spires of the cathedrals seemed false on the surface. Yet they attracted him more than almost anything else he saw. From the too-heavy spire of Salisbury Cathedral to the dripping forms of Antoni Gaudi's Church of the Holy Family encased by scaffolding and still to be finished, they pointed to some reality beyond this one, a transcendent reality that was not just abstract like Plato's Goodness, Truth and Beauty, or Aristotle's Unmoved Mover, or the Enlightenment's infinite but impersonal deity. They pointed to something much more like the biblical God, One who was above all, beyond all, knew all, could do all—all that he wanted to. And that was more than Jake could believe.

It's no use, he thought, and pondered returning to Kenton. He could at least return to his post, if not as chair (a job he didn't much like anyway), as a committed teacher of literature. He knew he would not teach Emily Dickinson as he had before. He would look differently on the great unwashed; he would see them as young men and women who one day would be faced with life and death, just as he had been. He would try to make literature prepare them for this profounder life.

He faced a decision. Do I give up and go home, stay in Europe in a small lonely apartment somewhere and live on early retirement, or continue my quest for emotional and intellectual relief? For days he pondered, visited art galleries, read poetry and pondered.

He faced a dilemma. If he was to overcome his grief with hope—hope in eternal life for his wife, hope for meaning on this earth for himself—he would have to break through an impasse. How could he do that without denying the very essence of what he had always believed? There might be a God, but if there is, it's an *it,* not a he or a she. Whatever God he could conjure up remained distant from human affairs. Could human reason alone be sufficient for framing a morality that transcended the morality of any given person or group? If so, humans would be doing God's work. Impossible. Human life ended in death. Well, maybe not totally; maybe there was some sort of continued existence of the soul, if not a fully personal existence at least one that preserved its goodness and intelligence.

But this truncated God didn't wash his daily laundry. It was not enough to satisfy his longing for a meaning and significance that affirmed his value here and now as a human being and preserved personality beyond the grave. Mary had to exist somewhere. She could not have simply dissolved along with her flesh and bones. *And death shall have no dominion,* he thought, but not because the dead are absorbed by the life spirit. There is no extension of personality here. Dylan Thomas must be wrong about that.

One thing the gory crucifixes showed, though, was that for Christian believers the body itself has value. Redemption, if there is such, includes the body. The resurrection shows that. The resurrected dead have bodies of some kind, and people live forever. Indeed *death shall have no dominion.*

He lay awake, his night thoughts swirling. Then, still in Madrid, he slept the deepest sleep he'd had since his wife fell ill. And in the morning he said, "I'm leaving. I'm going to the airport and taking the next plane out—not back to Ohio but on to the east—as far east as I can stand." This turned out to be Kiev. He had no idea what he would see. He just went.

As he always did, he browsed the English-language section of the airport bookstore. Delighted, he discovered six shelves of Penguin classics. He had not exhausted the treasures of his poetry anthology, but he had picked up an odd interest in the poetry of Gerard Manley Hopkins and the anthology included only a half dozen of his most anthologized poems. He wanted more. When he boarded the plane for Kiev, he had added Hopkins to his flight bag.

Three hours in the air and a dozen Hopkins poems read and reread, Jake arrived at Boryspil Airport, forty kilometers outside Kiev. As his taxi approached the city, the sunlit golden domes of a dozen ancient churches on bluffs overlooking the Dnieper River stood out against the horizon. This would be a place of beauty, he thought, even though its source was rooted deep in the pre-Marxist faith of the Ukrainians and Russians who had lived here for centuries. Communism was dead. Faith was being remembered and renewed. He knew that much. He chuckled to himself when he had chicken Kiev in the hotel restaurant; then he curled up with Hopkins again and slept, he thought the next morning, the sleep of the dead—no dreams, no night sweats, totally unconscious.

His newly refurbished room in an old hotel was large and comfortable. The taxi driver had recommended it in broken but adequate English. Jake guessed that the driver was in cahoots with the hotel and that both were probably run by the Ukrainian mafia, but he also knew that for visitors that was not a bad thing. You paid for it with higher rates, but it kept you safe. Moreover, the hotel was near the center of the city and the churches and museums he knew he wanted to visit. Much of his touring could be on foot.

The first morning he slept in, had breakfast in his room, channel-surfed the morning TV fare with its mostly European mixture in a half-dozen different languages, MTV, BBC, CNN and a European NBC. One of his friends had told him that ten years before, when he was in St. Petersburg, he had seen Jimmy Swaggart dubbed in Russian and the end of the last game of the World Series. Jake was pleased not to be so blessed. He shut off the TV and picked up his Penguin *Gerard Manley Hopkins.*

On the flight he had immersed himself in "God's Grandeur" with its glorious opening: *The world is charged with the grandeur of God,* its confession that humanity has not *recked his rod* but polluted earth with *man's smudge* and *man's smell,* and its glorious picture of the sun rising *because the Holy Ghost over the bent / World broods with warm breast and ah! bright wings.* What a touch, Jake thought, putting that *ah!* in the middle of the last line! And what an image of the dove of the Holy Spirit brooding and giving life to the giant egg of the earth! Here evil was acknowledged and overcome. No blank resignation and despair as in Stephen Crane, no gruesome contemplation of the dead who remain dead, no cheap, pious sentiment, just confidence in a God who redeems and restores.

Now he immersed himself in "The Starlight Night." *Look at the stars! look, look up at the skies!* In his mind Jake was transported to a starlit night. *O look at all the fire-folk sitting in the air!* Then Hopkins turns to the bright beauties of the earth, seen as a *purchase* (because of the blood of Christ?) and a *prize* (an unearned gift?). *Look, look: a May-mess, like on orchard boughs!* What does Hopkins want us to see? More, it seems, than meets the eye, though it is only through the eye, only because we look, that we see it at all. Yes, more than meets the eye, for the glorious earth is the *spouse / Christ home, Christ and his mother and all his hallows* (saints or angels). Jake is used to reading difficult poetry, but Hopkins has his own difficulties. He isn't sure precisely what Hopkins is saying, but even though he can't yet parse all the lines, he feels their meaning.

There is life in Hopkins's poetry, if he could only grasp it. He read and contemplated "The Sea and the Skylark," and then "Hurrahing in Harvest," and then "The Windhover," then "Pied Beauty," then "That Nature Is a Heraclitean Fire and of the Comfort of the Resurrection." He was bowled over. His heart was pounding. Counting the three hours on the plane, he had never spent this much time with Hopkins. Now Jake felt full of some sort of transcendent reality. He couldn't tour today. He was too full of wonderful images, mad thoughts of a world crammed with more than material, a world in which every element shouted at him: Look! See!

He had lunch, then walked around the central city and to the Great Gate of Kiev, a disappointment, he thought. Back at the hotel he rested, napped, actually had a snack in the coffee shop; then he walked again and returned for dinner. He'd rather liked the chicken Kiev, so he had that again. Then it was back to a nearby park, where he sat for a while, trying to see T. S. Eliot's evening *spread out against the sky / Like a patient etherized upon a table.* He couldn't do it. But then, neither could

C. S. Lewis, he recalled. What he could do, however, was read more of Hopkins. This time he turned to a whole set of poems he had been avoiding.

Hopkins had written a series known as the "terrible sonnets," not because they were bad poetry but because they expressed Hopkins's dark night of the soul, a feeling even the greatest of saints, perhaps *only* the greatest of saints, know. Sometimes the closer saints come to the most profound experience of God's presence, the deeper they experience God's absence.

No worst, there is none. He read. *Pitched past pitch of grief, / More pangs will, schooled at forepangs, wilder wring.* This was not *God's grandeur.* This was a grim reminder of his own grief. *Comforter, where is your comforting?*

My God, he thought, it isn't there. If there is no comfort for Hopkins, the priest, the one who sees Christ among the shocks of grain, even more so must there be no comfort for me. *Mary, mother of us, where is your relief?* No relief from God, none from the chiefest of saints.

> My cries heave, herds-long; huddle in a main, a chief—
> Woe, wórld-sorrow; on an áge-old anvil wince and sing—
> Then lull, then leave off. Fury had shrieked "No ling-
> ering! Let me be fell: force I must be brief."

Here *It* was again—not the sense of God's presence, not the stoic relief of resignation to Enlightenment reason, not the hope in union with Dylan Thomas's spirit of the cosmos. No, more like the nihilism and despair of Sylvia Plath's *nose, eye pits* and *teeth* that *vanish in a day.* Like Plath, Jake pondered: Must I be brief? Must I take my life? I must be gone? Here in Kiev where none of my friends knows where I am? Would this be the place to be gone forever?

> O the mind, mind has mountains, cliffs of fall
> Frightful, sheer, no-man-fathomed. Hold them cheap
> May who ne'er hung there. Nor does long our small
> Durance deal with that steep or deep. Here! creep,
> Wretch, under a comfort serves in a whirlwind: all
> Life death does end and each day dies with sleep.

Jake was already impressed with Hopkins's artistry, his "sprung rhythm" that enacts the sprung sense, the round-the-corner way of expressing his already round-the-corner slant truth. Now more and more he became impressed by Hopkins's grasp of the mountains and caverns of the human mind. Who would say *the mind, mind has mountains* but one who had himself hung on their cliffs? But Jake had already made up his mind that Hopkins was not mad, nor in writing these terrible sonnets had he abandoned his faith. It was because of his experience of God's presence that he could write so tellingly about God's absence.

He read one more "terrible sonnet": *Not, I'll not, carrion comfort, Despair, not feast on thee.* Here Hopkins wrestled directly with despair, refusing to give in to it, even when God laid a *lionlimb* against him or scanned *with darksome devouring eyes [his] bruisèd bones.* And he ends by realizing that after all the pain of the seeming loss of God, what comes is not a *formal feeling* but *chéer*, perhaps for both God and himself. The despair is gone. *That night, that year / Of now done darkness I wretch lay wrestling with (my God!) my God.*

There are echoes here of the opening lines of Psalm 22, lines Jake remembered from the Lenten sermons he'd heard when attending St. Andrews with Mary. Mary always insisted that once a year he at least get a sense of her spiritual journey through Lent. The lines had stuck with him, for they showed, as far as he was concerned, the despair of Jesus on the cross, something that seemed odd for the Son of God. But as he recalled the Lenten homily, Jesus' repetition of "my God" did show he had not been abandoned by God. Here, in different grammatical form, Hopkins made the same claim. Jesus was still in agony when he said the phrase; Hopkins had passed through his agony.

Jake had lunch again in the tourist hotel; he had not yet tired of eating off the land, so to speak. And he pondered his morning with Hopkins. Heavy, too heavy, he thought. Let's give me a break. So he went to the nearby national art gallery and was surprised to see how similar the paintings were to those he'd seen in Western Europe. There was, of course, a more Orthodox cast to the paintings of the saints and of Jesus, more ethereal, he thought, though he did not know quite why. And there was major attention to the work of Ukraine's modern artists. That work looked more Western than the earlier Christian art. Of course, he thought, it would. When the world becomes more modern, it becomes more Western. Dominant cultures swallow their weak competitors and transform their cultures. The layout of every recently built airport he had ever seen, for example, looked like every other one. Serious art, so it turns out, is not much different from kitsch.

Emotionally exhausted by the morning with Hopkins and physically tired from the gallery viewing, Jake returned to his hotel, had an early dinner and retired to his room. His mind, however, did not stop working. It began with memories of

Mary. How she would have loved what he saw this afternoon! How she had already appreciated Hopkins's poetry, especially "God's Grandeur" and "The Windhover"! Then his mind shifted to Hopkins's "terrible sonnets," and Ben Shahn's *The Man,* then back to the images of saints, the crucifixes and paintings of the passion of Christ he'd seen that morning. It was all a jumble. The pattern of his thoughts of Mary's death echoed the jumbled pattern of his reactions to poetry and painting. He could not put it all together. Something was missing. He longed for the sudden experience of peace and oneness that came from *Orange Abstract* and the sense of eternal timelessness and spacelessness inspired by the Zen rock garden. These were simple and final. Well, not finally final, for there was the return to the ordinary world. The many always surrounded the one. The many were real, the one then became either an illusion or a goal not yet achieved. He was beginning to think it was the former.

But that threw him back into his intellectual and emotional tussle with himself. Where was the really real? Was it the material world? No, there were too many signals of transcendence of both the positive kind ("Hurrahing in Harvest," for example) and the negative ("I wake and feel the fell of dark, not day"). The experience of ecstasy pointed to a good and loving God; the experience of agony pointed either to nihilism and the utter absurdity of the world or to the necessity of relief from a transcendent source. The Christian paintings, the cathedral spires and especially the poetry of Hopkins, dealt realistically with both the agony and the ecstasy. Nothing else did. Christian faith explained the presence of goodness in the world and why the world is no longer good. And more, it explained why there is still hope for human beings who do not despair but are confident that God somehow—through the incarnation, the life, death and resurrection of Jesus—has made atonement for human rebellion and failure. Through the power of his Holy Spirit, he broods over the bent world and is restoring all reality to its proper place in the kingdom of God. Moreover, Christian faith, even in its apparently paradoxical notions, is not irrational. One does not have to give up reason—only the autonomy of human reason. And even if one were to assert the power of unaided reason to reach truth, one might argue that the most reasonable understanding of the power of reason is that it is grounded in God, who has made us in his image.

Jake was ready for a moment of truth. He had it the next morning as he visited St. Volodymyr's Cathedral, the center of the Ukrainian Orthodox Church. He had no idea that this church had been constructed as recently as the nineteenth century and that its murals were not nearly so old as those he had seen in England and Spain. He also did not know that here he would *see* what he had not seen before.

He secured the help of a guide, a retired history teacher who claimed to know a great deal about the church and was anxious to dump all his knowledge on this American tourist. Soon he realized that Jake was no mere tourist uninformed about the Christian faith. His questions were not "How many tiles went into this huge mosaic?" Rather, they were honest and penetrating. The guide then changed his tone and, being something of an evangelist, gave Jake helpful answers to most of his questions. Jake, he thought, must be a Christian of some kind. He knew too much not to be. But he also sensed that Jake was not familiar with the Orthodox faith. He took Jake to the upper balconies and showed him huge murals, one of which, he was pleased to say, correctly identified the forbidden fruit as an orange, not an apple. Jake smiled.

The guide mostly wanted to contrast Orthodoxy and Western Christianity. He pointed to the emphasis on light from above and beyond in all the artwork—architecture, icons and paintings. Then he turned to Jake. "You capitalists, you Protestants and Catholics, are too interested in this world. We are interested in the coming kingdom of God, a realm not of this world but of heaven."

Jake had no reply. Well, he had a reply but he didn't use it. He took the point. Orthodoxy was obviously more mystical, more otherworldly, than either Catholicism or Protestantism. Neither was necessarily capitalist, but they did share with capitalism (and communism too, for that matter) an interest in the material world—its wealth and beauty. That was in fact what Jake had come to see. The Christianity he was exposed to in Western painting and especially the poetry of Hopkins was both earthly and heavenly. Without losing its earthiness, Earth itself was a sacrament. Even the hills displayed the *world-wielding shoulder* of Christ.

When Jake and the guide returned to the main door of the church, Jake looked up. Except for the inside of the large gold-plated door, a giant mural of the Last Judgment covered the entire back wall. Some fifty feet away, Jake stood and stared. The mural more than filled his vision. An eerie feeling came over him. This was *Orange Abstract,* the Zen rock garden and the whole body of Hopkins's poetry as he knew it. Here was not only the *aha!* sense that he stood in front of being itself; here was the meaning of being as well.

Jake's guide was now no help at all. He had no interest in the mural. He couldn't or wouldn't answer any of Jake's questions. Jake paid him and stood unmoving. Then he found a place to sit—difficult in an Orthodox church—and stared some more.

At the top of the painting the risen Christ sat as judge. Mary peeked over his shoulder; both had golden halos. On one side were the twelve apostles, on the other side the Old Testament patriarchs. A layer of clouds divided the heavens from the earth (below on the right side of Christ) and hell (below and on his left). In the center and directly above the door stood a giant angel with a scroll in his right hand and scales in his left. Two smaller angels, one to the right and one to the left of the angel of judgment, were blowing long trumpets.

On Christ's right the dead were rising from the earth to be judged by him. On Christ's left the damned were falling in excruciating pain into hell. A giant serpent, coiled and biting his own body, rose out of hell. Evil was destroying itself.

Jake never did get a professional analysis of this mural. But it wasn't necessary. Still in awe, he left the cathedral, found a bench overlooking a park and tried to sort out what had just happened. Something in him had changed. He *saw* for the first time just what Mary's Christian faith was all about. Mary did not need a trip to Europe or a visit to the great art galleries of the world. She did not need the poetry of Hopkins, though she loved it more than her husband had before these past few weeks.

In the following few days, Jake toured cathedrals even more striking than St. Volodymyr's. He saw the empty cells of ancient hermit monks. They were located along long corridors dug into the bluffs over the Dnieper River. But no church or monastery struck him as had this nineteenth-century church. Other churches did, however, begin to confirm in him what had leaped almost unbidden into his heart and mind. He had in some sense moved from unfaith to faith, from sophisticated deism to fledgling Christianity. His heart and mind had been changed. God had found him in St. Volodymyr's Cathedral in Kiev.

Hopkins now became his companion. He also began reading the Bible. Would you believe it—the Gideons had placed one, in English, in every room in his hotel. Then he bought one in the airport bookstore in Amsterdam when he had to change planes. He turned first to the Gospels, because he had seen that Christ was the key to understanding reality.

On his arrival at home, he went immediately to Mary's grave and wept. His tears were tears of grief and tears of joy. Where is Mary now? he had wondered. Now he knew. She was neither wholly in the grave nor wholly in heaven. She was awaiting resurrection, when she would be perfectly restored and able to reflect in glory the glory of God.

Jake again recalled these marvelous lines from Hopkins's "That Nature Is a Heraclitean Fire and of the Comfort of the Resurrection." In his mind he put Mary in the place of Hopkins and said out loud:

Flesh fade, and mortal trash
Fall to the residuary worm; I world's wildfire, leave but ash:
In a flash, at a trumpet crash,
[She is] all at once what Christ is, I since he was what [she is], and
This Jack, joke, poor potsherd, I patch, matchwood, immortal diamond,
Is immortal diamond.

"Amen," Jake said as heart and mind soared to meet her and their Savior Jesus Christ.

ARGUMENTS FROM EVERYTHING

"Night Thoughts and Day Dreams" is fiction, an example of narrative apologetics. Is it literature? Does it fit all the criteria of the definition given in chapter four? The author did try to fulfill some of the criteria. The story creates a Secondary World. In the Primary World there is no Jean-Jacques LeRoi, no wife Mary, no Kenton College. There is Ohio, London, Madrid, Ukraine, Kiev. All the poems and artworks referred to exist. The Primary World includes all those.

"Night Thoughts and Day Dreams" is a story, not a simple discourse, a logical argument or a speech designed to persuade. The plot is an oldie. Is it archetypical? Maybe. Is the story a product of poetic intuition? Possibly. Or it may be only a long, mechanically contrived illustration of the doctrine of salvation. Presumably the author wants it to be an imaginative narrative apologetic for traditional Christian faith. He speaks for himself.

I have tried to make Jake LeRoi's journey from a modest form of deism to Christian faith illustrate the place the visual arts and poetry play in my own reasons for continuing to believe. I did not make such a journey. I was already a believer when I first encountered serious poetry, and serious art came even later for me.

Still, a few comments may clarify what I call "the argument from Goya."

The arts are signals of transcendence; they point to the existence of some-thing nonmaterial. They cannot be fully explained by materialistic assump-tions, for they arise from the deep wells of the human imagination informed by the deep foundation of an artist's worldview. One can avoid such signals of transcendence only by ignoring or suppressing them.

Taking a solely aesthetic approach to their appreciation is one major way of not seeing beyond their artistic excellence. Before his wife died, that's how Jake responded to the literature he loved. This approach, however, can be falsified by crisis, by a breakthrough from beyond, in short, by the Holy Spirit working through the ordinary circumstances of life. In Jake's case the crisis was the death of his wife. When he read poetry after this, he realized that the best poets were not being solely aesthetic in their own approach to the world. They were not just making art objects. Whether they knew it or not, they were enacting in their art their own take on life. Being true to one's vision, being honest to one's readers, makes it impossible to be solely mate-rialistic or pantheistic or deistic or even nihilistic. Every stroke of the brush says no to nihilism. Every painter putting oil on canvas reveals something of herself that is not to be explained by anything but the existence of a tran-scendent and, I believe, not to be fully explained by anything other than a full-fledged Christian worldview.

In chapter two I presented Peter Berger's notion of signals of transcen-dence and listed several of them—ordering, hope, damnation, humor and play. The first section of the book delineated signals that I have detected in my own experience; the present section deals with signals that are triggered by literature and painting. There are other signals I will not discuss but just suggest. From science, for example, there is the complexity of the universe, the fine-tuning of the constants that hold it together and make human life possible, the seemingly irreducible complexities of the biosphere.[5]

Some readers may find it odd that I include so many signals that involve darkness rather than light—Hopkins's terrible sonnets, Goya's black paintings, Dickinson's quiet but unsatisfying skepticism. There are two reasons for this. First, these dark episodes in our lives—our depressions, represented and sometimes triggered by dark paintings and anguished poetry—are usually thought of as arguments against the existence of a God who is not all-powerful or not all-good or not all-knowing, or not any of the three. This is not the case, for the very existence of our sense of evil and the injustice of at least some of our suffering is best explained by the existence of a God who grounds our sense of the good in his transcendent reality.

Second, we are more likely to be impressed with pain than with pleasure. When we are more or less happy, we tend to forget the God who has made us capable of experiencing happiness. We attribute that pleasure to our own goodness or righteousness or cleverness or intelligence. We deserve it, we tell ourselves. The fact is that we do not. Every good thing that comes to us comes by God's grace. Pain and suffering remind us of this.

Many years ago, when I first imagined the outline for the story of Jake's conversion, I did not have a detailed theology that would attempt to represent all the factors that led to his conversion. I do now. The process began with a profound crisis. Then many signals of transcendence were strewn along the way, some pointing this way, some another. Reason and revelation were bound together as Jake pondered the meaning of his experience. There was fascination and horror, loneliness and frustration, memory and musing. There was willy-nilly progress and setback. Eventually as he looked back, Jake could see a meaning in the puzzling turns of the journey. But when his profound shift in worldview happened, it seemed to him to be both sudden and radical. It was like the last hundred pieces of a five-hundred-piece jigsaw puzzle automatically and suddenly slipping into place to reveal the whole picture.

However, the faith his wife had lived and enjoyed turned out to be the truth Jake sensed but had suppressed. Jake had run to Europe, and God had caught up with him.

As it turns out, our world is so fashioned and has such a history that it is no exaggeration to say that every person is created for Christ and everything created makes a case for Christ.

7

MEETING THE UNEXPECTED

The Argument from Jesus

Philip found Nathanael and said to him, "We have found him
about whom Moses in the law and also the prophets wrote,
Jesus son of Joseph from Nazareth." Nathanael said to him,
"Can anything good come out of Nazareth?"
Philip said to him, "Come and see."

JOHN 1:45-46

IN CHAPTER THREE ABOVE, I suggested that a properly Christian defense
of faith could be presented in a three-pronged apologetic approach based
on the reality of God:

1. An argument from God, not to God

2. An argument from everything to God

3. An argument from our personal experience—direct perception—of God
   in everything

Is this approach being realized by the flow of the argument in this book?
Let's take a look.

First, and in a very important sense, every proper human argument is an
argument based on God. Were it not for God's existence, there would be no

one to argue and no arguments to be made. Atheists, deists, pantheists, nihilists—from a Christian point of view—are, whether they know it or not, God's creation. So from this standpoint there is no avoiding "arguing from God." So arguments 2 and 3 in this book and elsewhere involve argument 1. A case for this absolute ontological starting point is found in chapters one and two.

Arguments 2 and 3 are necessarily interwoven. After all, argument 2 implies there is a person to experience the "everything." And argument 3 implies that there is an "everything" to experience. Chapters three through six interweave these two sorts of argument.

So, yes, the book so far has illustrated its stated organizational thesis. But there is one more dimension to argument 1—an argument from God. God presents himself to us both in words and in the Word made flesh. We, on the receiving end, experience him both indirectly and directly. We can, then, argue from God because God has given himself to us. As he does that, he allows us to perceive him and thus complete a type 3 argument.

The argument from the God who reveals himself in his words through the prophets and through his intimate presence with us is the most important argument. It is the last, best argument of all. So we turn to that now.

Everything in Christ astonishes me. His spirit overawes me, and his will confounds me. Between him and whoever else in the world, there is no possible term of comparison. He is truly a being by himself. . . . I search in vain in history to find the similar to Jesus Christ, or anything which can approach the gospel. Neither history, nor humanity, nor the ages, nor nature, offer me anything with which I am able to compare it or explain it. Here everything is extraordinary.

—Napoleon, quoted by Philip Yancey, *The Jesus I Never Knew* (Grand Rapids: Zondervan, 1995), p. 83

"COME AND SEE!"

If I were to give only one reason for continuing to believe in Jesus Christ, it would be Jesus himself. It may then seem odd that I have left it for the last.

Well, Jesus himself said that the first shall be last and the last first, though he surely did not have this example in mind.

The last is first for several reasons, the most important of which is that Jesus Christ is the final reality that I am trying to understand. If I meet him, if I encounter him person to person, if I respond to that encounter by confessing my unworthiness to be in his presence, if I say yes to him and continue in his Word, obeying him and living a life that reflects his character in my character, then I am truly his disciple. I do not merely have good information about him, a good argument for his being the be-all and end-all of reality or a grasp of his being the Creator-Redeemer himself. Rather, I am directly engaged with the really real, the final reality, ultimate reality itself in all its personal dimensions. This, then, is not knowledge *about*; this is knowledge *of.*

UNMEDIATED KNOWLEDGE

When our hearts turn to him, that is opening the door to him, that is, holding up our mirror to him; then he comes in, not by our thought only, *not in our idea only, but he comes himself and of his own will.* Thus the Lord, the Spirit, becomes the soul of our souls, becomes spiritually what he always was creatively; and as our spirit informs, gives shape to our bodies, in like manner his soul informs, gives shape to our souls.

In this there is nothing unnatural, nothing at conflict with our being. It is but that the deeper soul that willed and wills our souls, rises up, the infinite Life, into the Self we call *I* and *me,* makes *I* and *me* more and more his, and himself more and more ours; until at length the glory of our existence flashes upon us, we face full to the sun that enlightens what is sent forth, and know ourselves alive with an infinite life, even the life of the Father. Then indeed we *are*; then indeed we have life; the life of Jesus has, through light, become life in us; the glory of God in the face of Jesus, mirrored in our hearts, has made us alive; we are one with God forever and ever.

—George MacDonald, *Creation in Christ,* quoted in Rueben P. Job and Norman Shawchuck, *A Guide to Prayer for Ministers and Other Servants* (Nashville: Upper Room, 1983), p. 267

Knowledge of does not require a conscious epistemology, an understanding of how it is that I know him. This knowing is immediate, unmediated, without contract. It is not what some mystics are seeking—a pantheistic merging of the soul with God. But it is something that anyone can actually achieve: an intimate and personal knowledge of God himself.

Another way to put this is to say that all manner of ordinary and extraordinary things on earth are or can be signals of transcendence. Jesus is not that. He is not a signal of anything. He's it. He is Reality. Jesus the Christ is the One in whom "we live and move and have our being" (Acts 17:28). Jesus is not so much the *reason* (epistemology) as he is the *reality* (ontology). We drop all attempts to think about how we know a person when we are wrapped up in his or her life. After all, as Os Guinness says, "There is more to human knowing than human knowing will ever know."[1] Some of it is, as Plantinga puts it, palpable.[2] We feel it in our bones. But much is tacit. We know it, but we don't know how we know it.

Perhaps an example will help. If you ask me who my wife is or what she is like, I can certainly tell you lots of things about her. But if you encounter her, all this information drops into the background. It is not that it has been useless or false. It may be neither. It may be why you decided to seek her out. But when you see her for yourself, you no longer need my introduction.

Of course you do not know everything I know, and some of what you think you know about her may be incorrect. Some of what I know may also be incorrect. We humans are like that. We think we know lots of things we don't. But we can grow in our knowledge by direct participation with those we have met.

MEETING THE UNEXPECTED JESUS

I first met Jesus simply as *my Savior*. That was long ago. But Jesus is much larger than my first and most basic experience of him. I now meet Jesus daily, especially as I read Scripture, not only the Gospels but Paul's letters and the Old Testament as well. And whom do I find? Ah, that is one of the most exciting and rewarding parts of Scripture reading. I never know before reading what will dawn on me and become an active part of my encounter with Christ.[3]

Of course, Jesus is much larger—infinitely larger—than my current experience of him. He is the most unexpected figure in history. He astounded everyone he encountered. I have written about Jesus in more detail else-where.[4] Here I will only sketch the outlines of my understanding.

On the one hand, as the Messiah he was expected by the Hebrew people, not just the prophets but the psalmists who longed for a solution to the troubled life of Israel and the troubled souls of its people. But when he arrived as Messiah, he puzzled everyone. The Jews of his day knew that God would ultimately solve the problem of sin. But their understanding of how he would do this was not only limited but wrong.

Psalm 22, for example, posed a problem. How is God to forgive our sins and still justly judge us for them? We do not learn the answer till Jesus has died and is resurrected. Even then we have to wait till his apostles learn through his postresurrection teaching and tell Jesus' other followers what has really happened.

Psalm 22, which Jesus quotes as he hangs on the cross, begins this way:

My God, my God, why have you forsaken me?

After an agonizing twenty verses of intensifying lament, the psalm ends in ten verses of ecstatic praise as the psalmist calls on everyone to praise the Lord. From old to young, rich to poor, from Israel to the ends of the earth, from his own day to the end of time, everyone will praise God. Why this radical shift from despair to delight?

Only Jesus, as he quotes its first and last lines on the cross, solves the riddle (Mark 15:34).[5] Only the resurrection of the divine Son who has been forsaken by his divine Father could justify the ecstatic praise that the final verses of Psalm 22 call for.

On the other hand, when Jesus came, the people of Israel, especially those who should have recognized him, did not see him as the Messiah. He constantly upset their expectations. The Messiah was supposed to release Israel from its captors—the Assyrians, the Babylonians, the Romans. Jesus was not bent on doing this. Instead he claimed to forgive sins (Mark 2:5), something the Messiah was not expected to do. Nor was he expected to be a healer or an authoritative interpreter of the Hebrew Scriptures.

With his teaching in the Sermon on the Mount (Matthew 5–7) Jesus challenged the religious leaders on a host of ethical issues. Take, for example, murder (anger is as reprehensible), justice (loving one's enemies), leadership and honor (the last will be first), sin (a matter of the heart, not just one's actions) and the proper response to evildoers (no retaliation). He accused his fellow townsmen of unbelief, likened himself to Moses, Isaiah, Elijah and Elisha, and was kicked out of his own hometown (Luke 4:18-30). He offended his fellow Jews by making a Samaritan, rather than a priest or a Levite, a model to imitate (Luke 10:25-37).

When he was asked questions, he often replied with either a question or a story, sometimes both, as he did in the story of the good Samaritan just cited. Moreover, his stories were not just clever tales to illustrate a point; they were parables that demanded a decision from the listeners. When the story was over, those who listened either moved from unfaith to faith or, as in the parables of the good Samaritan (Luke 10:25-37) and the prodigal son (Luke 15:11-32), were left dangling. Like the elder son in the story, they could either accept Jesus, who hobnobbed with sinners, or stay out in the field, far from the salvation pictured by the festivities for the return of the younger son. The religious leaders found his stories offensive because they recognized that they had been the butt of Jesus' unexpected criticism. If they were to follow Jesus, they would have to radically change their take on the Hebrew Scriptures and life itself.

When they asked why he had the authority to interpret Scriptures so differently from them, he posed for them a dilemma. The result was that they would have to either accept his authority or put themselves in physical jeopardy with the general populace (Mark 11:27-33). They wanted to do neither; so, declining to be impaled on either horn, they left without an answer. Only those willing to obey could know *how* they should obey.

One of Jesus' most astounding characteristics is the natural, almost casual way he displays his divine character. He did not often declare in so many words that he was the Son of God or equal to God. He let his actions and his engagement and dialogues with people display who he was. He did this in such a way that if we pay attention and are open to seeing, we cannot miss the implication that Jesus thought of himself as—and displayed himself to be—someone with a very special relation to God.

Take one of the early events in Jesus' life as Mark recounts it in Mark 2:1-12. Jesus had been traveling in Israel and had returned to his home in Capernaum, a town on the north shore of the Lake of Galilee. So many people had gathered there that the room in which he was teaching was packed. Four men then came carrying a paralyzed friend on a cot. When they couldn't get in, they went to the roof of the house—house roofs in Galilee were flat—and opened it up and let the man down in front of Jesus. Jesus, recognizing the faith of the four, looked at the paralyzed man and said, "Son, your sins are forgiven."

Now, think about it. Was this the reason he had been brought to Jesus—to have his sins forgiven? Surely he and his four friends must have been surprised and disappointed. One can imagine them wanting to say, "Jesus, that's not what we want. We want him healed. We've heard that you have the power. Won't you do that for our friend?" But before they can respond, the religious leaders who are there begin to ponder: How Jesus could claim to forgive sins? Isn't that the prerogative of God alone? They were right, of course; only the one sinned against can forgive that sin. The man had not sinned against Jesus; he had sinned against God.

Jesus knew what these religious leaders were thinking. So he asked them, "Which is easier, to say to the paralytic, 'Your sins are forgiven,' or to say, 'Stand up and take your mat and walk'?" Well, we think as readers, both of them sound quite impossible!

But Jesus quickly added, "But I want you theologians and everyone to know that I have authority on earth to forgive sins. So, you there on the cot, rise, take up your pallet and go home" (my paraphrase). And the man did just that.

The response of the crowd was utter amazement. "We have never seen anything like this!" they said.

But the amazement was due not primarily to Jesus' power to heal. There had been other healers in Israel. It was Jesus' implicit claim to have the power and the authority to forgive sins that people found shocking. By the time the disciples were made fully aware of who Jesus was—the very Son of God, the One whose death on the cross paid for the sins of the paralyzed man and all humankind—they would see that it was completely reasonable and appropriate for Jesus to say, "Your sins are forgiven." But at the time, what a mystery it must have been!

There was no question in the disciples' minds that Jesus was an ordinary man who walked as they walked, got tired and thirsty as they did, attended synagogue and prayed as they prayed. But there was also no question that Jesus was someone very special, with a consciousness of the presence of God that they longed for but did not possess. On the one hand, he was an ordinary teacher, teaching many of the truths they knew or were reminded of from Scripture. In some ways he taught like the rabbis, asking questions, preaching (as in the Sermon on the Mount in Matthew 5–7), telling stories. On the other hand, he often taught in ways that were unique. Many of his stories were not like the stories of the rabbis. At the end of these stories those whom he addressed were forced to respond by changing their behavior, not just their beliefs.

Jesus was, of course, the first and so far the only human being to be resurrected. Many apologists, especially those of my generation, emphasize the apologetic implications of this unique event. They see it as the coup de grâce to disprove purely naturalistic explanations. Jesus must be more than a mere material being. The resurrection witnesses to his divinity. Moreover, if Jesus rose from the dead, we should listen to him. He must be not only a unique person but both our Savior and our Lord.

I do not so much reject this argument as I find that it misses the point. The point is not the wonder of his resurrection so much as the wonder of Jesus. He is more amazing than his resurrection. The resurrection does not so much confirm the truth of the gospel as it becomes the reasonable fulfillment of Jesus' mission and revelation of his divine-human nature. We should look back on the resurrection and say, "Of course Jesus rose from the dead. He has shown himself to be the only person who could have done so. It fits his character; it is the reasonable conclusion to his life. It fulfills his mission and demonstrates why his claim to forgive sins is utterly reasonable." The disciples should have known this because Jesus himself said it would happen and showed by raising people from the dead that at least he could do that. Of course, they would die again and he would not. And today we certainly should affirm his resurrection, because his disciples testified to it, even though one of them (Thomas) had such a hard time doing so.

Another way to see Jesus and the resurrection is to see the event of the resurrection as a brilliant, boisterous, seemingly undeniable signal of transcendence and the resurrected Jesus himself as the reality to which it points. But as we know, its meaning and significance can be suppressed. How responsible must we be for suppressing such truth!

Over and over as I read the Gospels I am given a greater grasp of who Jesus really is. Of course, I cannot grasp him in his infinite entirety; I can see only what he allows me to see—the Infinite revealing to the finite something of his glory.[6] But it is enough to keep me aware of his presence and to keep me coming back to Scripture more and more, attempting more and more to obey what I come to see as his will, confessing my continuing shortcomings and sins, moving forward from forgiveness, and straining, as the apostle Paul said, to reach the goal he has for me. In other words, in keeping in contact with Jesus I have come to know Jesus as my Lord.

ENIGMAS RESOLVED

When we encounter Jesus, we have before us Reality himself. If Jesus Christ is the reality and not just the sign of something deeper, then he should be the answer to the enigmas of human experience. That is what I have found. In him is the solution to all the puzzles that we would like to solve. There are many of these enigmas. But for me, the first enigma Jesus addressed was the enigma of sin and salvation.

The enigma of sin and salvation. Very early in life I knew about my sins, though I might not have called them that. In fact, I don't remember when the term itself became part of my active vocabulary. Sin was, of course, an active part of my life. My first information about Jesus came with my mother's Sunday school teaching and from *The Lutheran Hour* and Charles Fuller's program on the radio. I learned more from the few country school-house church services I attended. But the whole story about sin and salvation through Christ did not sink in until the summer before the seventh grade. That's when Pastor Ward Smith made the simple gospel clear and I met Jesus as my Savior.

All the subsequent sermons I heard, all the talks given by Youth for Christ speakers, all of Mrs. Tomek's Sunday school teaching, all my subsequent Bible study, often with my InterVarsity student colleagues, and all the books I've read have added to my head knowledge of Jesus. But the reality of the relationship with Christ begun sixty some years ago and extending till today is my first and foremost reason for continuing my commitment to Christ. If there were no other reason for my faith than this, it would be enough. But let me give some details to strengthen the case.

The account of sin and forgiveness given in Scripture fits with absolutely all my experience. Psalm 32, which parses the relationship between sin and forgiveness, is lived out on the nerve endings of my life:

> While I kept silence [about my sins], my body wasted away
>   through my groaning all day long.
> For day and night your hand was heavy upon me;
>   my strength was dried up as by the heat of summer. (vv. 3-4)

I felt that as a young boy. I still feel it today:

> Then I acknowledged my sin to you,
>   and did not hide my iniquity;
> I said, "I will confess my transgressions to the LORD,"
>   and you forgave the guilt of my sin. (v. 5)

Confession, genuine repentance and the desire to turn away from repeated sinning still bring the sense of forgiveness and a reaction of joy.

> You are a hiding place for me;
>   you preserve me from trouble;
>   you surround me with glad cries of deliverance. (v. 7)

Precisely then, years ago. Precisely now, age eighty and still going, and so far increasing.

The psalmist then gives the advice I have always needed for daily living:

> Do not be like a horse or a mule, without understanding,
>   whose temper must be curbed with bit and bridle,
>   else it will not stay near you. (v. 9)

The principle, stated early and repeated at the end, is simply this:

> Happy are those whose transgression is forgiven,
>   whose sin is covered.
> Happy are those to whom the LORD imputes no iniquity,
>   and in whose spirit there is no deceit. . . .
> Many are the torments of the wicked,
>   but steadfast love surrounds those who trust in the LORD. (vv. 1-2, 10)

And the final word of Psalm 32 is a word of worship, the only fitting response when I reflect on my status before God. When I met Jesus—first in the pew when I fainted, and then at the front of Butte Community Church—I could not have explained this, but, no matter, I experienced it. Before this I was only a sinner, a person made in the image of God but broken by sin. Now I was a sinner saved by grace. Thus the importance of the final verse of the psalm:

> Be glad in the LORD and rejoice, O righteous,
>   and shout for joy, all you upright in heart. (v. 11)

The enigma of the cross. There are several perspectives from which we can view the enigma of the cross. On the one hand, we ask, why did Jesus, the very Son of God, the Creator of the heavens and the earth, the perfect God and perfect man, have to die? It seems unjust. On the other hand, we puzzle, how could an all-righteous God who will stand for no evil forgive our sins? He can't just say, "There, there, it's all right. Everything will be all right." That is to trivialize evil. Yet, like the mother comforting her child, that is just what God does.

The reality of the crucifixion and resurrection solves this enigma. The all-righteous God who has created a good universe has given a part of that creation the opportunity to make a decision not just to *be* good but to *do* good, to obey God's perfectly righteous will. But human beings, though created in his image, chose to disobey, causing a rift between God and his creation. There is only one way to restore humankind's relationship with God. That is for God himself to become human as Jesus Christ and take the place of his rebellious creatures before God's own court. God himself bears our sin. In doing so, Jesus Christ cries out to the Father, "My God, my God, why have you forsaken me?" (Mark 15:34). Then Jesus is resurrected, and his act of atonement, of reconciling God and humanity, shows that his sacrifice—the separation in the Trinity of the Son from the Father—is sufficient.

In Christian art and iconography, the crucifix becomes the empty cross, and both are turned into beautiful art. The enigma of the cross is solved.

The enigma of evil. This enigma is profoundly addressed by the cross. How could a good and omnipotent God create a world in which some of his creation will forever be separated from him? If God is good, he would not do this. He must not be really good, or not really omnipotent, or, perhaps, not really intelligent. The reality of the crucified Christ shows that God has made every provision for all who will turn to him to avoid eternal separation. They need only acknowledge their rebellion and call on the grace of God.

God is vindicated, and we are saved from permanent separation from God.

The enigma of suffering. This is a piece of the larger enigma of evil. Here the question is, why do the innocent suffer? They do so, of course, because they participate in the corporate body of humanity. What affects the whole affects the part. Each of us suffers due to not only our own sinfulness but also that of others. It all seems so unjust. And, indeed, it may well be unjust for the moment. But eternity will compensate for even the most unjust suffering. This we hold in hope because we have seen Christ suffering on the cross—unjust because he doesn't deserve it, but more than just, rather utterly loving, from the standpoint of God's grace. Again Jesus Christ is the reality that solves the enigma.

The enigma of human nature. Jesus Christ is also the final reality resolving the enigma of human nature—our glory and our wretchedness. Blaise Pascal has said it well: "What sort of freak then is man! How novel, how monstrous, how chaotic, how paradoxical, how prodigious! Judge of all things, feeble worm, repository of truth, sink of doubt and error, glory and refuse of the universe!"[7]

One day this mixture of the commendable and the despicable will be separated, either by sanctification or by degradation. As C. S. Lewis said, "It is a serious thing to live in a society of possible gods and goddesses, to remember that the dullest and most uninteresting person you talk to may one day be a creature which, if you saw it now, you would be strongly tempted to worship, or else a horror and a corruption such as you now meet, if at all, only in a nightmare."[8] How can we be transformed into the all glorious? Why do we not all descend to the pit?

Jesus Christ, the Second Adam, showed us human perfection. But he also became the wretched of the earth as he took on himself all the sins of the world. He became sin so that we need not take the reasonable consequence of our sin—separation from God. Today we are a mixture—wretched and glorious. But one day we will either be entirely wretched or become as we were intended to be—utterly glorious. Jesus is the reason.

The enigma of human reason. We have seen in chapter one that human reason often seems to work very well, but not always and never thoroughly. Moreover, even when it works it doesn't do so on its own. Human reason is not autonomous. Again, the reality of Christ untangles the puzzle.

Christ is the foundation of human reason. He is the Logos, the Word, the reason, the meaning, the intelligence of God. And as the Creator he is the reason that the cosmos is itself reasonable, orderly, not the chaos of the Greek myths, not the airy-fairy impersonal spirit of pantheistic religions, not the unknown and unknowable plenum void of Buddhism.[9] Then, too, as the Logos, he made us in his image, and even broken as it is, there is reason to use our reason.

The enigma of body and soul. Christ also solves the enigma of body and soul. In the previous chapter I pictured Jake LeRoi at the grave of his wife Mary. His experience is an almost exact description of my own (or vice versa?).

My mother died in a hospital in Des Moines, Iowa, but she was taken to the small town of Butte, Nebraska, for burial. When our family arrived, her body lay in an open casket in the town's only funeral parlor.

We walked into the room on a warm day in May 1984. I looked at the casket and saw my mother briefly—a glance really. My wife Marj followed me into the room, saw the sad look on my sister's face and suddenly collapsed. All attention turned to Marj. We got her to a chair and decided it was best for her to go to the family home. I would, I thought, see my mother again at the church funeral the next day. That would be normal, I thought. But not in Butte. When I arrived at the church, the casket had been closed for the final time. All through the service, both at the church and at the hillside cemetery, I felt something was missing. I had not said goodbye. I had not stood by my mother's coffin as I had at the wakes and funerals of many of my friends. She was gone. I had not dealt with the fact that she was really dead, that I would never see her again on earth. I simply had not said goodbye.

After the funeral, I left Dad, her friends and my relatives at a reception at my parents' home. I drove alone back to the cemetery and stood by her grave. A soft wind blew across the grave, which had already been filled in. I stood looking at the grave, looking at the big Nebraska sky, pondering. Why hadn't I gone back to the funeral parlor? Why didn't I say goodbye?

Then I wondered, Where is my mother? She is in the grave. No, she isn't; she's in heaven. No, she isn't; here in front of me lies her body in a casket, covered by rich Nebraska soil. No, that's not my mother; there's no life there. She's in heaven. No, not yet, not completely so.

Never did the resurrection of Jesus and his teaching of the resurrection of the body make more sense to me. Here was the answer to the enigma of what a human being is. Body and soul, or soul embodied, a unity of body and soul, both together, not one without the other. My mother's death, the funeral and my being at her grave were together a signal of transcendence. There is more to life than a functioning but decaying body; there is a permanence to every human being. There is a resurrection of the dead. There is a life eternal. There has to be. Nothing makes sense without this. And in the Christian faith, Christ, the firstfruits of the resurrection, is the reality to which this particular signal of transcendence points.

THE BIBLE AS LITERATURE

It may seem odd that I have not yet mentioned the argument from the Bible as the Bible. This has been by design. Of course I could not have met Jesus without the Bible. Nor could I believe in anything particularly Christian if I did not believe the Bible was the authoritative Word of God, that the history it tells is reliable, and that its teaching about God, humanity and the universe is true. But I take this to be a secondary, perhaps even tertiary, matter.

A STORY OF A LARGER KIND

The Gospels contain a fairy-story, or a story of a larger kind which embraces all the essence of fairy-stories. They contain many marvels—peculiarly artistic, beautiful, and moving: "mythical" in their perfect, self-contained significance; and among the marvels is the greatest and most complete conceivable eucatastrophe [happy ending]. But this story has entered History and the primary world; the desire and aspiration of sub-creation has been raised to the fulfillment of Creation. The Birth of Christ is the eucatastrophe of Man's history. The Resurrection is the eucatastrophe of the story of the Incarnation. This story begins and ends in joy. It has pre-eminently the "inner consistency of reality." There is no better tale told that men would rather find was true, and none which so many skeptical men have accepted as true on its own merits. For the Art of it has the supremely convincing tone of Primary Art, that is, of Creation. To reject it leads either to sadness or to wrath.

—J. R. R. Tolkien, "On Fairy-Stories," in *The Tolkien Reader* (New York: Ballantine Books, 1966), pp. 71-72

Before I explain why, I must say something about what the Bible is. First, the Bible itself is a work of ancient literature. Too often well-meaning Christians read it as if it were written like a modern history or a list of things to believe, or as a book of laws and rules, or as a work of systematic thought—theology or philosophy or, worse, science. The Bible is, rather, a collection of a wide variety of literary types. It must be read as it was intended to be read by those who wrote it and by its ultimate author, God himself, who has spoken through writers to lead his people into a deep love of God. Reading the Bible as literature (with literature defined as in chapter 2) will yield amazing results.

That means each text must be read as it comes to us (through, indeed, the scholars and translators). I give only one illustration of this. To read the Gospel of John as if it were what we today call biography or history is a mistake. It contains biography and it speaks of historical events, but a Gospel is a unique form of literature, one suiting its time and place. We find out what it is not by forcing it to meet our expectations but by paying the closest attention to what it is before us.

Early in the 1960s, when I read Merrill C. Tenney's *John: The Gospel of Belief,* my basic understanding of how to read Scripture changed.[10] Tenney read the Gospel of John as a unit defined by its own structure. He did not read it from the standpoint of a predetermined theology; he derived its theology from the structure and content that was there. I found the same careful "literary" reading in John Marsh's commentary *The Gospel of St. John* in the Penguin/Pelican series. How different is the approach of Raymond Brown in *An Introduction to the Gospel of John* in the Anchor Bible Commentary series! He sees the Gospel as a tissue of pieces patched rather unskillfully together and is more interested in leaving the Gospel of John in pieces from which little authoritative information can be gained.

One of the reasons that the Bible is the Word of God to us is that it comes with its own literary structure—a structure of many structures, each making its own contribution to the task of bringing us back into a deep relationship with God in Christ. As a signal of transcendence, the Bible is a giant beacon. But we must not use it to show us what we want to know. We must let it show us what God wants us to know. Read it for that. It will give us more than we ever deserve to know.

The reality we want to know is not a book or the teaching of a book. We want to know reality itself, not the authoritative witness to reality, no matter how inspiring or how inerrant.

LIFE WITH THE BIBLE

My own early intimations of immortality, my first signals of transcendence, were not from the Bible but from my life on the rim of the Sandhills of Nebraska: the hills and rivers, the thunderheads and ice jams, the life and words of my parents, grandparents and country friends. I grew to know there was something more than this material world. I was taught by Pastor Smith, who taught from the Bible, before I knew much about the Bible, and certainly before I had seriously studied it.

Still, the Bible is the source of my most basic beliefs about God, humanity and the universe. It is not unimportant to ask why I came to accept this authority and still do.

My first reason for believing the Bible was that it was considered by my family to be the authoritative Word of God. But soon another reason became primary—my sense that the Bible is utterly realistic. There are puzzles, things I still don't comprehend, but where I do, I find it fits the world as I know it. E. E. Cummings once wrote, "I say the world not fit you." Yes, but the Bible does. And the fact that the world doesn't fit us is itself a signal of transcendence. It makes us ask, What does fit us? Every aspect of us? When we plumb the Bible, we find out.

I have written three books that focus on the Old Testament, one near the beginning of my writing career and two near what I presume will be the end. During the politically and culturally troubled 1970s, I became fascinated by the prophet Jeremiah. The book of Jeremiah first appears to be a pastiche of obscure prophecies and partial accounts of Jeremiah's life. For me it was a challenge to understand. But with the help of commentaries, I discovered its astounding relevance to that decade. Out of that observation came a set of group Bible studies titled *Jeremiah, Meet the Twentieth Century* (1975). The method here was inductive and primarily involved the use of the mind.

I had long counted the fulfillment of biblical prophecy as a weak argument for the reliability of the Bible. It seemed too easy to account for fulfilled prophecy as imaginative reading of Old Testament texts, squeezing out of them meanings they didn't have when they were spoken. Prophecy predicted events; history unfolded to show the prediction correct. There is, indeed, some of this sort of prophecy in Scripture. But rather dramatically for me, while writing my two books on the Psalms, I changed my mind. This is not the only way prophecy is meaningful. In fact, it is not the most important way. Here's how I found out.

My encounter with Psalm 22 was nothing less for me than a major signal of transcendence. There was the psalmist, crying out to God because of being abandoned and left to suffer. This made sense as a human experience. But when the psalmist, after receiving relief, calls on everyone—past and present and future, across all social classes, all across the world—to praise God for saving him, and by extension the tiny nation of Israel, something clicked in my mind. The psalmist seems overly impressed with his own value. Neither his salvation nor the salvation of his nation merits this ecstatic outpouring of praise.

But when I noticed that Jesus did not quote only the opening phrase, "My God, my God, why have you forsaken me?" but also the final phrase, "he has done it" (v. 31), or "it is finished" (John 19:30), it became clear to me that Jesus was incarnating the entire psalm—beginning to end—in his experience on the cross. He was fulfilling Psalm 22, and only he could do it. For his death was a death for all of us. His resurrection was a resurrection for all of us. Of course, then, the call for ecstatic praise is right and proper, the only rational thing for everyone at any and all times to exclaim.

Thus as I began the process of studying and contemplating the Psalms, I came to an entirely different understanding of the prophetic passages in the Old Testament. I gradually came to see them as, in the final analysis, christological. Jesus as a young boy and youth began to pick up the themes of the Hebrew Scriptures and see that something was missing. Some of the prophetic passages needed fulfillment. Somehow, he then saw that his role was to fulfill the messianic longings. Deliberately he set out to embody them. As a consequence, my grasp of the reliability of Scripture has taken on a much stronger foundation.

Let me add a third reason: my own experience of Bible reading itself has become *sacramental*. This may not be the best word. I'm not sure what that word might be. I often sense the presence of God as I read. By no means is this always the case. Sometimes the text seems to be only words, words, words—no meaning, just empty words. At other times the words take on life, spring from the page, sometimes grand and beautiful, sometimes striking terror. In every case, they become signals of transcendence: God is here, right here in my conscious presence. He is looking into my mind, stirring my emotions, enlightening my mind, prompting me to attend now and forever to his presence in worship and stimulating me to obedience and to living in his light. Of course the Bible is God's faithful revelation of himself, at the moment, especially to me.[11] How could that not be?

In the late 1990s I was introduced to *lectio divina*, which involves reading, rereading, then, without asking questions of the text, letting it sink below the level of consciousness. From that deep well, connections can be made that are not noticed in the more typical inductive way of asking (1) what does the text say? (2) what does it mean? and (3) what is its application to today? The inductive process has merit; it reflects the modern university's proper emphasis on reasonable reading. But sometimes it misses the direct impact that Scripture can have on our present conscious mind.

My two recent books *Learning to Pray Through the Psalms* (2005) and *Praying the Psalms of Jesus* (2007) involve all three approaches: (1) a brief elaboration of the christological reading of the Psalms, (2) *lectio divina* and (3) more academic methods of reading.

An earlier book on the Bible, *Scripture Twisting* (1980), was inspired by my frustration with the gross misreadings I was finding in the cult books and pamphlets that I read as background to books I was editing for Inter-Varsity Press. Their writers made me angry, perhaps also a signal of transcendence, an evil presence in their words.

The Bible is utterly realistic. Its view of people in general fits me in particular. It reads me like a book. When it describes its "heroes," they are believable—honorable but flawed, oriented toward God but rebellious and foolish, called like King David to serve God at the highest level but falling into the sins of adultery and murder. But while Jesus is so human that his own disciples did not recognize his divinity until after the resurrection, he is so godlike, so perfect, that those same disciples eventually came to see him as God himself in human form.

For me the Gospels are the most important witness, the brightest signal, to the reality of Christ. Jesus' words and actions are themselves self-authenticating. Jesus must have been as he is described. No one could out of their imagination create a character like him. If he had not already been, there would be no one like him in any literature. Yet in spite of his uniqueness, he emerges out of the pages of the Gospels as the most real person we have ever met.

We try to understand him. Then we find that he understands us better than we understand ourselves. We read the Gospel of Mark, for example, suddenly stop reading and say, "Who is this guy?" Then we read more and ponder. We are struck by what we come to see. Finally, we find ourselves compelled either to bow and say, "My Lord and my God," or to walk away sadly or in anger.

I am all too aware of the objections to the reliability of the Bible, especially the Gospels. Over the years I have read many of the books—most of the most significant ones—that counter and try to suppress my traditional Christian view. And I have read the scholars who have met these challenges and concluded that the Bible is indeed trustworthy.[12] So I need say no more in defense of Scripture. It speaks for itself much better than I can speak for it. In any case, it is the divine-human Jesus Christ who himself bears the best testimony to the final truths of reality.

Jesus, the unexpected Jesus, the unique Jesus, the One who makes sense of all of reality: he is the first and final reason for my commitment to him. Come and see!

AFTERWORD

> ◆ <

THIS BOOK BEGAN BY ASKING: Is there an apologetic—a case for Christ—
that "lays before the watching world such a winsome embodiment of the
Christian faith that for any and all who are willing to observe there will be
an intellectually and emotionally credible witness to its fundamental truth"?
If there is one, what is it? This took us on a journey—a personal one for me.
I asked you to go along. To hear what I've heard. To see what I've seen.

I hope you will have seen these things. First, all our arguments as Christians should begin with God. That is, it should begin with our confidence
that the One who created us made us able to know. We trust God, not our
own unaided reason. Second, this confidence in God is supported by God's
presence with us, in us, in ourselves, in our lives. Signals of God's presence
are all around us. We need primarily to pay attention and to follow those
signals where they lead.

Signals of the extraordinary come in every dimension of life. When we
have attuned our lives to listen, we see the glory of God everywhere. Here
we could have looked at the amazing phenomena of nature, at the revela-
tions of the work of scientists, the transfixing of our souls as we listen to
great music, the beauty of the human face from birth to death. Despite my
silence in this book about many of the forms of rational apologetics, the
works of brilliant Christian theologians and philosophers, if we were to look
at them as signals of the really real and not as intellectual "proofs" relying
on assumptions we share with unbelievers, we would add even more depth
to our apologetic. The cleverness of all clever arguments is a signal of the
image of God. Of course we must not ignore our God-given reason. We
must use it to put the meaning of the signals into their place in our developing grasp of God. Let us use rational apologists to help us put our intuitive

grasp of God—our sense of his presence—into significant intellectual form. Let us expect our experience to result in a deepening orthodox faith in God.

My hope is that the literature and poetry we've examined shows some of the depth of meaning in God's signals. I hope we have seen that not only do Hopkins and Milton give glory to God, but, despite their failure to see it, so do Stanislaw Lem and Virginia Woolf.

Signals of transcendence—so many, so powerful, so glorious, so wooing, so beautiful, so present in everything. So mindful, so mystical, so obvious, so mysterious. And then Reality!

Jesus, the incarnation of God, is the ultimate Reality to which all the experiential and biblical signals point. He strides with quiet dignity through the Gospels, shaking up the Hebrew, Greek and Roman cultures, challenging men and women with impossible ethical principles, telling stories that lay the listeners low or strike them with hope almost beyond belief.

Think of Job and Ruth. Think of the eclectic variety of challenges to God's reality and the reality of his creation. Think of the metanarrative from "In the beginning" to Maranatha: "Amen, come, Lord Jesus." Think of the gradual revelation of who God is and what he desires and how his intentions will be fully realized.

But don't get stuck on the signals. Turn your eyes upon Jesus the Christ, Son of the living God, Prince of Peace, our Savior, our Lord and our elder Brother. Seeing really is believing.

Let us say to the watching world: "Come and see!"

NOTES

Preface

[1] Peter Kreeft and Ronald Tacelli, *Handbook of Christian Apologetics* (Downers Grove, IL: InterVarsity Press, 1994), p. 81. Long ago Kreeft and Tacelli set me thinking about the implications of their "argument from Bach." The several forms this argument takes in this book should show how much it has meant to me.

Chapter 1: The Past as Prologue

[1] Saul Bellow, *Mr. Sammler's Planet* (New York: Fawcett World Library, 1970), p. 216.

[2] James W. Sire, *A Little Primer on Humble Apologetics* (Downers Grove, IL: InterVarsity Press, 2006), p. 26.

[3] The *kalam* argument is a version of the first-cause argument for God's reality developed by Islamic thinkers; it claims that the world must have a beginning and that God must exist as the cause of that beginning. See William Lane Craig, *The Kalam Argument* (New York: Barnes and Noble Books, 1979); and J. P. Moreland and William Lane Craig, *Philosophical Foundations for a Christian Worldview* (Downers Grove, IL: InterVarsity Press, 2003), pp. 468-80.

[4] Confession time! This assumption that rational arguments should convince even when they don't is a theme that runs through my own contribution to *Deepest Differences* (Downers Grove, IL: InterVarsity Press, 2009), which I wrote with atheist and scientist Carl Peraino.

[5] C. Stephen Evans, *Despair: A Moment or a Way of Life?* (Downers Grove, IL: InterVarsity Press, 1971).

[6] See especially Os Guinness's *The Dust of Death* (Downers Grove, IL: InterVarsity Press, 1973) and *The Gravedigger File* (Downers Grove, IL: InterVarsity Press, 1983).

[7] I have omitted from the following biographic autobiography several books that are outside the normal category of apologetics. My first book was coauthored with my colleague Robert Beum when both of us were teaching English at Nebraska Wesleyan University. *Papers on Literature: Models and Methods* (1970) was designed as a text for sophomore writing classes. *Jeremiah: Meet the 20th Century* (1975) was a Bible study guide for small groups. *Beginning with God* (1981) derived from the confirmation classes I taught for seven years. Its role was to introduce basic Christianity; the pastor's role was then to introduce the Presbyterian Church. *Discipleship of the Mind* (1990) was an expanded comment on the Christian worldview and its relevance to academic life.

[8]*The Universe Next Door* is now in its fifth edition (2009). The preface explains some of the many worldview changes in New Age forms of pantheism and postmodern forms of naturalism, and the increase of relevance of Islam in the West.

[9]A description of the rhetorical form and content of this lecture can be found in "On Being a Fool for Christ and an Idiot for Nobody: Logocentricity and a Postmodern Apologetic," in *Christian Apologetics in the Modern World*, ed. Timothy R. Phillips and Dennis L. Okholm (Downers Grove, IL: InterVarsity Press, 1995), pp. 101-27.

[10]The title reflects my admiration for John Stackhouse's *Humble Apologetics: Defending the Faith Today* (New York: Oxford University Press, 2002).

[11]Two books reflecting my love for the Psalms, *Learning to Pray Through the Psalms* (2005) and *Praying the Psalms of Jesus* (2007), involve three approaches: (1) a brief elaboration of the christological reading of the Psalms, (2) *lectio divina* and (3) more academic methods of reading.

[12]Readers of both books will find similar, sometimes identical, commentary on two of Hopkins's poems ("God's Grandeur" and "I wake and feel the fell of dark"), Virginia Woolf's novel *The Years* and other occasional casual comments. The two books were completed at nearly the same time, and this duplicated commentary is necessary to the argument of each. Cascade Books and InterVarsity Press have granted permission for this common text.

[13]I wonder how many of us walk away after our talks and conversations thinking we have failed. This disappointment may say more about our lack of humility than we'd like to think.

Chapter 2: Wondering About God

[1]Blaise Pascal, *Pensées*, trans. A. J. Krailsheimer (Harmondsworth, UK: Penguin, 1966), no. 449, p. 170.

[2]Pascal, "The Memorial," in ibid., no. 913, p. 309.

[3]René Descartes, "Discourse on the Method," in *The Philosophical Works of Descartes*, trans. Elizabeth S. Haldane and G. R. T. Ross (New York: Dover, 1955), p. 101.

[4]Bernard Ramm, *Witness of the Spirit* (Grand Rapids: Eerdmans, 1960). See as well C. Stephen Evans, *Faith Beyond Reason: A Kierkegaardian Account* (Grand Rapids: Eerdmans, 1998); the first three chapters are especially helpful.

[5]*Proper confidence* is Lesslie Newbigin's term for what as Christians we can expect from thinking and experience within the framework of a Christian worldview. See his *Proper Confidence: Faith, Doubt and Certainty in Christian Scholarship* (Grand Rapids: Eerdmans, 1995). I have learned as well from Alvin Plantinga and Nicholas Wolterstorff and their colleagues in *Faith and Rationality: Reason and Belief in God* (Notre Dame, IN: University of Notre Dame Press, 1983).

[6]I am aware that there are several ways the word *presuppositional* is used, but I prefer the simple definition I give here. I have presented this conception in greater detail in *Naming the Elephant* (Downers Grove, IL: InterVarsity Press, 2004), pp. 79-86.

[7]The use of *best explanation* (abductive reasoning) is not a capitulation to rationalism or the autonomy of human reason. It is rather a guard against believing from blind faith.

[8]Richard Dawkins from a book review in the *New York Times*, April 9, 1989. My own view of evolution is explained in *Why Good Arguments Often Fail* (Downers Grove, IL: InterVarsity Press, 2006), pp. 92-105. See as well *The Universe Next Door,* 5th ed. (Downers Grove, IL: InterVarsity Press, 2009), pp. 81-83.

[9]Bertrand Russell, *Problems in Philosophy* (New York: Oxford University Press, 1912; often reprinted).

[10]Nietzsche has a devastating critique of Descartes's statement "I think; therefore I am" and what Descartes says follows from it. See Friedrich Nietzsche, "Beyond Good and Evil," in *Basic Writings of Nietzsche,* trans. Walter Kaufmann (New York: Modern Library, 1969), pp. 213-14. My more detailed critique of Descartes's I-think argument and his four arguments for the existence of God will be found in *Naming the Elephant,* pp. 55-56.

[11]Stanislaw Lem, *The Cyberiad,* trans. Michael Kandel (New York: Avon, 1976; original Polish editions 1967 and 1972). Page numbers for all quotations from this book will hereafter be provided in parentheses.

[12]See Lem, "The World as Cataclysm," in *One Human Minute,* trans. Catherine S. Leach (New York: Jovanovitch, 1986), pp. 72, 96.

[13]Jacques Monod, *Chance and Necessity,* trans. Austryn Wainhouse (New York: Alfred A. Knopf, 1971).

[14]Lem, "One Human Minute," p. 72.

[15]Ibid., p. 96.

[16]Ibid., p. 102.

[17]In his novels such as *The Futurological Congress, Memoirs Found in a Bathtub* and *The Chain of Chance,* Lem constructs a world in which this sort of nihilism is systemic. Much of his writing is comic, but it is humor directed toward keeping him sane in an insane world.

[18]See my *Naming the Elephant,* pp. 58-67, for a more detailed critique of Descartes's argument.

[19]Descartes, "Meditation II," in *The Philosophical Works of Descartes,* p. 152.

[20]True, Descartes later argues that God's existence undergirds his own and that like his own idea of himself, the idea of God is innate, but only after he has proven from the fact of his own existence that such a God exists. See Descartes, "Meditation III," in *The Philosophical Works of Descartes,* p. 170. For Descartes and the rationalists, epistemology precedes ontology.

[21]Ramm, *Witness of the Spirit,* pp. 36-38.

CHAPTER 3: IN THE BEGINNING

[1]Helmut Thielicke, *Nihilism: Its Origin and Nature—with a Christian Answer* (London: Routledge and Kegan Paul, 1961), pp. 32, 36, 46, 65.

[2]James W. Sire and Carl Peraino, *Deepest Differences* (Downers Grove, IL: Inter-Varsity Press, 2009), pp. 19-41, 113, 149-53, 179-80.

[3]Thomas Nagel, *The Last Word* (New York: Oxford University Press, 1997), p. 130. In *Intimate Diaries,* the existentialist philosopher Miguel de Unamuno made a similar remark: "I have always fought against dogmatism, allegedly for the sake of freedom, but in reality it was because of pride so that I wouldn't have to fall in line or recognize something else as superior or discipline myself"; quoted by Jan E. Evans, *Miguel de Unamuno's Quest for Faith* (Eugene, OR: Pickwick, 2013), p. 15.

[4]Sire and Peraino, *Deepest Differences,* pp. 173-83.

[5]John Calvin, *Institutes of the Christian Religion,* trans. Henry Beveridge (London: James Clark, n.d.), 1.v.1.

[6]Readers who want to see how Christians handle these criticisms may consult dozens of books. See, for example, those listed in the bibliography at the end of this book.

[7]Those who assume the autonomy of human reason usually assume that Christians are assuming the same thing. Of course Christians may be doing so, but they certainly don't need to and shouldn't.

[8]The particular approach I am taking with this argument for "beginning with God" derives, I suspect, in part from an exposure to Reformed epistemology as elucidated by Alvin Plantinga. See especially his *Warranted Christian Belief* (New York: Oxford University Press, 2000), pp. 167-98. I read this book and other articles by Plantinga some time ago, and by now it just seems to me to be true. As Plantinga himself says, "If Christian beliefs are true, then the standard and most satisfactory way to hold them will not be as a conclusion of an argument" (p. 201); one just sees that they are so. This does not, however, mean that they are self-evident. It is more a matter of direct perception, a sort of God-given *sensus divinitatis* for perceiving truths of the natural world. If this is not what Plantinga means, okay: it's what I mean.

Jacques Maritain explains the immediate intuition of God and one's being in the world from the stance of neoscholastic philosophy: "Before entering into the sphere of completely formed and articulated knowledge, in particular the sphere of metaphysical knowledge, the human mind is indeed capable of a prephilosophical knowledge which is *virtually metaphysical.* Therein is found the first, the primordial way of approach through which men became aware of the existence of God" (*Approaches to God,* trans. Peter O'Reilly [New York: Macmillan, 1954], p. 18).

[9]"To the believer," Plantinga says, "the presence of God is often *palpable*" (*Warranted Christian Belief,* p. 181).

[10]For a one-page blog listing multiple signals prompting belief in the biblical God, see Walter Russell Mead, "The Meaning of Christmas," *The American Interest,* December 29, 2013, http://us-mg205.mail.yahoo.com/neo/launch?.partner-sbc&rand=erop9gnjsvfsd.

[11]Benjamin Wiker and Jonathan Witt examine a host of ordinary (but amazing) phenomena from literature, physics, mathematics and biology that point powerfully toward the likelihood of design in the universe and consequently to a Designer outside the universe. See *A Meaningful World: How the Arts and Sciences Reveal the Genius of Nature* (Downers Grove, IL: InterVarsity Press, 2006).

[12]Peter Berger, *A Rumor of Angels* (Garden City, NY: Anchor Books, 1970), p. 57. More recently a number of Christian apologists have cast attention on such signals of transcendence. Among them are Os Guinness, who focused some of his graduate work on Peter Berger. See his *Long Journey Home: A Guide to Your Search for the Meaning of Life* (Colorado Springs: Waterbrook, 2001), p. 50; N. T. Wright, *Simply Christian: Why Christianity Makes Sense* (San Francisco: HarperSanFrancisco, 2006), p. 225; and John M. Templeman and Robert L. Hermann, *The God Who Would Be Known* (San Francisco: Harper & Row, 1989), pp. 1-2. For a profound theological analysis of the numinous and the *mysterium tremendum,* perhaps the most significant of all signals of transcendence, see Rudolf Otto, *The Idea of the Holy,* trans. John W. Harvey (Harmondsworth, UK: Penguin Books, 1959 [orig. German, 1917; first English ed., 1923]), p. 129. I first read Otto's book thirty or forty years ago; recently it has had a profound influence on my understanding of the direct perception of God.

[13]Berger, *Rumor of Angels,* p. 47.

[14]Berger discusses these four signals of transcendence in ibid., pp. 52-75.

[15]My explanation of humor is a simplified take on Berger's more complex analysis.

[16]Virginia Woolf and some of her fictional characters experienced "moments of being"; these have some of the same characteristics as signals of transcendence, but she, being a vocal atheist, would have nothing to do with genuine transcendence. She describes these in "A Sketch of the Past" in *Moments of Being,* 2nd ed., ed. Jeanne Schulkind (New York: Harcourt Brace, 1985), pp. 70-73.

[17]See, for example, Rob Mole's comments on Albert Camus in "Saved by an Atheist," *Christianity Today,* August 2010, and David Haddon's comments on Jack London's "Never Beyond Zero," *Touchstone,* February 2009.

[18]"Inductive faith" is the term Berger uses to label the epistemological transaction leading from a signal of transcendence to the perception of this transcendence. That is, signals of transcendence are not in any strict sense *proofs* that what they point to necessarily exists (Berger, p. 60). What Berger calls *inductive faith* is the sort of engagement we have with reality when we see our brother and recognize who it is we have seen.

[19]John Hundley, "Becoming a Thoughtful Christian in the Secular Academy: Part II," *InterVarsity Emerging Scholars* blog, June 27, 2013, http://blog.emergingscholars.org.

[20]My *Echoes of a Voice* (Eugene, OR: Cascade, 2014) is being published at the same time as the present book. It deals in depth with the nature and character of signals of transcendence and the ways they are understood within the frameworks of the worldviews just listed.

[20]Saul Bellow, *Mr. Sammler's Planet* (New York: Fawcett World Library, 1969, 1970), p. 216.

CHAPTER 4: SECONDARY WORLDS

[2] [1]C. S. Lewis, *Surprised by Joy* (London: Geoffrey Bles, 1955), pp. 23-24.

[3] [2]I was delighted recently when rereading *Experiment in Criticism* (London: Cambridge University Press, 1961), p. 93, to find that C. S. Lewis chastises teachers thus: "Especially poisonous is the kind of teaching which encourages [students] to approach every literary work with suspicion."

[4] [3]I realize my attempt to fashion a "theory" of literature may be audacious. I remember one literary critic (I think it was Hazard Adams) who deliberately refused to do so.

[5] [4]My interpretation of this poem has evolved over the years, and I am unable to document the sources of all I say here. The translation is from Donald Keene, *Japanese Literature: An Introduction for Modern Readers* (Tokyo: Charles E. Tuttle, 1955), p. 39.

[5]Other translators have certainly not noticed Bashō's attempt to convey the soundlessness of the precise interface between frog and water. See Hiroaki Sati's *One Hundred Frogs* (New York: Inklings/Weatherhill, 1995).

[7] [6]*The Complete Poems of Emily Dickinson*, ed. Thomas H. Johnson (Boston: Little, Brown, 1960), poem 341, p. 162.

[8] [7]Jacques Maritain, *Creative Intuition in Art and Poetry* (New York: Meridian Books, 1955), pp. 80-85.

[9] [8]Aesthetic experience, aesthetic value and a host of other complex issues of the philosophical discipline of aesthetics have, for me, been best articulated and evaluated by Monroe C. Beardsley in *Aesthetics: Problems in the Philosophy of Criticism* (New York: Harcourt, Brace and World, 1958).

[10] [9]Joseph Conrad, preface to *The Nigger of the Narcissus* and *The End of the Tether* (New York: Dell, 1960), p. 27.

[11] [10]Yvor Winters, "Poetry, Morality, and Criticism," in *The Critique of Humanism: A Symposium*, ed. C. Hartley Grattan (New York: Brewer and Warren, 1930), p. 301.

[12] [11]Conrad, preface, p. 25.

[13] [12]Stephen Crane, untitled poem, in *The Complete Poems of Stephen Crane*, ed. Joseph Katz (Ithaca, NY: Cornell University Press, 1972), p. 22.

[14] [13]Friedrich Nietzsche, "The Madman," section 125 in *The Gay Science*, in *The Portable Nietzsche*, trans. Walter Kaufmann (New York: Viking, 1954), pp. 95-96.

[15] [14]See Roger Lundin's in-depth study *Emily Dickinson and the Art of Belief* (Grand Rapids: Eerdmans, 1998).

[16] [15]In *Complete Poems of Emily Dickinson*, poem 1129, pp. 506-7.

[17] [16]Maritain, *Creative Intuition*, p. 87.

[18] [17]A Dickinson saying that Col. Higginson wrote in a letter to his wife; see *Masters of American Literature*, ed. Henry A. Pochmann and Gay Wilson Allen (New York: Macmillan, 1949), 2:409.

[18]The four basic terms of this diagram come from M. H. Abrams, *The Mirror and the Lamp* (New York: W. W. Norton, 1958; orig. ed. 1953), p. 6.

[19]Some readers may be confused by my use of the terms *Primary World* and *Secondary World*. I adapted them from Tolkien, who used it them in "On Fairy-Stories," in *The Tolkien Reader* (New York: Ballantine Books, 1966), to describe the fantasy world of fairy tales. I have expanded the scope of the concept to include any "world" created by a literary work in either poetry or prose.

[20]William Irwin Thompson, *The Edge of History* (New York: Harper and Row, 1971), pp. 27-30.

[21]Lewis Carroll, "Jabberwocky," in *Through the Looking Glass*, in *The Annotated Alice*, with notes by Martin Gardner (New York: Clarkson N. Potter, 1960), pp. 191-92. Gardner's notes in this edition of both *Through the Looking Glass* and *Alice in Wonderland* are a gift to all lovers of Lewis Carroll.

[22]Ibid., pp. 271-73, and notes on pp. 191-97.

[23]Peter Berger says, "Indeed the most fundamental assumptions about the world are mostly affirmed by implication—they are so 'obvious' that there is no need to put them into words" (*A Rumor of Angels: Modern Society and the Rediscovery of the Supernatural* [Garden City, NY: Anchor Books, 1970]), pp. 36-37.

[24]See my *Naming the Elephant: Worldview as a Concept* (Downers Grove, IL: InterVarsity Press, 2004), p. 122. This book is a defense of this definition.

[25]For William F. Lynch's neo-Thomist explanation of analogy and how in literature the transcendent need can be best represented by the immanent, see Lynch, *Christ and Apollo: The Dimensions of the Literary Imagination* (Wilmington, DE: ISI Books, 2004), esp. pp. 13-45 and 179-215.

[26]Conrad, preface, 26.

[27]The form of this chart bears some resemblance to Maritain's charts in *Creative Intuition in Art and Poetry*, pp. 219-20.

[28]Tolkien, "On Fairy-Stories," p. 37.

[29]Conrad, preface, p. 29.

[30]What I am suggesting here is a method of reading much like the medieval *lectio divina*, though literature in general has none of the divine authority of the Bible. I have discussed this in *Habits of the Mind: Intellectual Life as a Christian Calling* (Downers Grove, IL: InterVarsity Press, 2000), pp. 152-63. See also Michael Casey, *Sacred Reading: The Ancient Art of Lectio Divina* (Liguori, MO: Triumph Books, 1996). C. S. Lewis's entire *An Experiment in Criticism* (London: Cambridge University Press, 1961) is a masterful explanation of good reading.

[31]For more detailed instructions, see my *How to Read Slowly* (Colorado Springs: Shaw Books, 1978).

[32]Lewis, *Experiment in Criticism*, p. 136.

[33]Ibid., p. 137.

35 ³⁴Ibid., p. 139.
36 ³⁵Ibid., p. 141.

CHAPTER 5: BRIGHT WINGS AND WOBBLING LIGHTHOUSES

[1]John Milton, *Paradise Lost*, 1, lines 1-6. To newcomers to this epic, I recommend the publication edited by Merritt Y. Hughes (New York: Odyssey, 1962): the editor's notes are superb. The most helpful full introduction is C. S. Lewis, *Preface to Paradise Lost* (London: Oxford University Press, 1962).

[2]Gerard Manley Hopkins, "God's Grandeur," in *The Poems of Gerard Manley Hopkins*, ed. W. H. Gardner and N. H. MacKenzie, 4th ed. (London: Oxford University Press, 1967), p. 66.

[3]Hopkins, Sonnet 67, in *Poems*, p. 101.

[4]In her novels Woolf almost always treats Christians, Christian doctrine and Christianity in a negative way, and occasionally is even hostile. Take this passage from *Night and Day*: "So large is the church, and in particular the church tower, in comparison with the little street of cottages which compose the village [of Dishham], that the traveller is apt to cast his mind back to the Middle Ages, as the only time when so much piety could have been kept alive. So great a trust in the Church can surely not belong to our day, and he goes on to conjecture that every one of the villagers has reached the extreme limit of human life" (*Night and Day*, ed. Julia Briggs [London: Penguin, 1992], p. 148).

[5]David Daisches, *Virginia Woolf* (Norfolk, CT: New Directions Books, 1942), p. 4.

[6]Pages from Virginia Woolf, *Jacob's Room* (New York: Penguin Putnam, 1998), will be cited following each quotation.

[7]William Shakespeare, *Othello*, act 5, scene 2, line 7.

[8]The phrase "mobile army of metaphors" is Nietzsche's, apt here because, as in Nietzsche, truth is totally perspectival, dependent on the time, place, culture and person, and thus ontologically insubstantial. See "On Truth and Lie in the Extra-moral Sense," in *The Portable Nietzsche*, trans. Walter Kaufmann (New York: Viking, 1954), p. 46.

[9]Pages from Virginia Woolf, *The Years* (New York: Harcourt Brace, 1937), will be cited following each quotation.

[10]Virginia Woolf, "Modern Fiction," in *The Common Reader: First Series* (New York: Harcourt Brace Jovanovich, 1925), p. 154.

[11]Ibid., p. 155.

[12]Virginia Woolf, "A Sketch of the Past," in *Moments of Being*, 2nd ed., ed. Jeanne Schulkind (New York: Harcourt Brace, 1985), p. 72.

[13]The French reads in translation: The mediocrity of the universe astonishes and revolts me. . . . The pettiness of all things fills me with disgust. . . . the poverty of human beings destroys me.

[14]Peter Kreeft and Ronald Tacelli, *Handbook of Christian Apologetics* (Downers Grove, IL: InterVarsity Press, 1994), p. 81.

[15]This same message is given form in the parable of the sower (Luke 8:4-15) and the parable of Lazarus and the rich man (Luke 16:19-31).

[16]John Calvin, *Institutes of the Christian Religion,* trans. Henry Beveridge (London: James Clark, n.d.), 1.1.1-5; and Plantinga's explanation in chap. 3, n. 8, above.

[17]Abraham Kuyper, *Lectures on Calvinism* (Grand Rapids: Eerdmans, 1931).

[18]Friedrich Schleiermacher, "Second Speech: The Nature of Religion," in *On Religion: Speeches to Its Cultured Despisers,* trans. John Oman (London: K. Paul, Trench, Trubner, 1893), Kindle edition.

CHAPTER 6: NIGHT THOUGHTS AND DAY DREAMS

[1]I don't know the precise title of this painting; moreover, it seems no longer to be listed in the Sheldon collection, and it is not reproduced in Bernarda Bryson Shahn's *Ben Shahn* (New York: Harry N. Abrams, 1972). But I am describing a Ben Shahn painting as I remember it. Many of Shahn's paintings, notably *Cosmos* (1956) and *Anger* (1953) (pp. 26 and 96), are in the general style of the one I remember but not quite as dark in mood. Shahn's *Trouble* (1947), depicting a fight between two men with a roller coaster in the background, is still held by the Sheldon Memorial Art Gallery at the University of Nebraska.

[2]I have no idea what title was given to this painting or who the artist was. But I had such an *aha!* experience when I was a student delivering educational films to professors at the Morrell Hall art gallery.

[3]I visited El Prado in the mid-1990s and saw all the paintings of Velázquez and Goya that I mention here. I have also consulted these books to refresh my memory: Jonathan Brown, *Velázquez: Painter and Courtier* (New Haven, CT: Yale University Press, 1986); Richard Schickel and the editors of Time-Life Books, *The World of Goya, 1746-1828* (New York: Time-Life Books, 1968); Francisco-Xavier de Salas Bosch, *Goya,* trans. G. T. Culverwell (Danbury, CT: MasterWorks, 1978); Sarah Symmons, *Goya* (London: Phaidon, 1998); and Robert Hughes, *Goya* (New York: Alfred A. Knopf, 2003).

[4]With regard to the young woman, I am following here the interpretation of Schickel and the editors of Time-Life, *World of Goya,* p. 183.

[5]See Benjamin Wiker and Jonathan Witt, *A Meaningful World: How the Arts and Sciences Reveal the Genius of Nature* (Downers Grove, IL: InterVarsity Press, 2006).

CHAPTER 7: MEETING THE UNEXPECTED

[1]Os Guinness, *In Two Minds* (Downers Grove, IL: InterVarsity Press, 1976), p. 41.

[2]Alvin Plantinga, *Warranted Christian Belief* (New York: Oxford University Press, 2000), p. 181.

[3]I rarely choose one book as very best of its kind. But I make one exception. The best book introducing Jesus to anyone—non-, new or old believer—is Philip

Yancey, *The Jesus I Never Knew* (Grand Rapids: Zondervan, 1995).

[4]See *Why Should Anyone Believe Anything at All?* (Downers Grove, IL: InterVarsity Press, 1994), pp. 110-63.

[5]See my *Praying the Psalms of Jesus* (Downers Grove, IL: InterVarsity Press), pp. 23-33.

[6]I am reminded of Schleiermacher's language quoted above (p. 97): Jesus is "a revelation of the Infinite in the finite."

[7]Blaise Pascal, *Pensées,* trans. A. J. Krailsheimer (Harmondsworth, UK: Penguin, 1966), no. 131, p. 64.

[8]C. S. Lewis, "The Weight of Glory," in *Transposition and Other Addresses* (London: Geoffrey Bles, 1949), p. 32.

[9]I have written more about this aspect of Christ as Logos in *The Discipleship of the Mind* (Downers Grove, IL: InterVarsity Press, 1990), pp. 78-95.

[10]Merrill C. Tenney, *John: The Gospel of Belief* (Grand Rapids: Eerdmans, 1960).

[11]Bernard Ramm, citing Calvin, says this: "The Bible itself teaches . . . that when God gives his revelation, he gives along with it a certainty that it *is* revelation." *Witness of the Spirit* (Grand Rapids: Eerdmans, 1960), p. 12.

[12]See the bibliography section "The Historical Reliability of the Bible," p. 157.

BIBLIOGRAPHY

IN THE PRESENT BOOK I have focused on the role of experience in apologetics, primarily through signals of transcendence. This is not because I wish to dismiss or shortchange rational and evidential approaches to the difficult and complex task of justifying our claim that Christianity is true—exclusively true in every case where it is contradicted by alternatives. Every sort of valid reasoning and deep experience is valuable in the defense of faith.

There is, indeed, a huge library of excellent works of apologetics; its holdings extend back as far as Eusebius, Tertullian and Augustine and forward as far as the latest volume from my contemporaries. In *Why Good Arguments Often Fail* (2004) I compiled an annotated list of significant works of apologetics. That was ten years ago, but though many excellent books have been added since then, it's still worth consulting for its panoramic sweep.

Here I will be much more selective, listing only the best of the best as I judge them today. If you start with these, you will be building your growing grasp of apologetics on strong foundations.

Backgrounds and Foundations of Apologetics
Campbell-Jack, W. C., and Gavin McGrath, eds. *New Dictionary of Christian Apologetics*. Downers Grove, IL: InterVarsity Press, 2006.

Moreland, J. P., and William Lane Craig. *Philosophical Foundations for a Christian Worldview*. Downers Grove, IL: InterVarsity Press, 2003.

Sire, James W. *The Universe Next Door*. 5th ed. Downers Grove, IL: InterVarsity Press, 2009.

Groothuis, Douglas. *Christian Apologetics: A Comprehensive Case for Christian Faith*. Downers Grove , IL: InterVarsity Press, 2011.

The Reasonability of Christian Faith

Chamberlain, Paul. *Why People Don't Believe: Confronting Seven Challenges to Christian Faith*. Grand Rapids: Baker Books, 2011.

Clark, David K. *Dialogical Apologetics: A Person-Centered Approach to Christian Defense*. Grand Rapids: Baker Books, 1993.

Copan, Paul. *Is God a Moral Monster?* Grand Rapids: Baker Books, 2011.

Edgar, William. *Reasons of the Heart: Recovering Christian Persuasion*. Grand Rapids: Baker Books, 1996.

Evans, C. Stephen. *Why Believe: Reason and Mystery as Pointers to God,* rev. ed. Grand Rapids: Eerdmans, 1996.

Keller, Timothy. *The Reason for God: Belief in an Age of Skepticism*. New York: Dutton, 2008.

Kreeft, Peter, and Ronald K. Tacelli. *Handbook of Christian Apologetics: Hundreds of Answers to Crucial Questions*. Downers Grove, IL: InterVarsity Press, 1994.

Lewis, C. S. *Mere Christianity*. New York: Macmillan, 1952.

McGrath, Alister E. *Mere Apologetics: How to Help Seekers and Skeptics Find Faith*. Grand Rapids: Baker Books, 2012.

Pascal, Blaise. *Pensées*. Translated by A. J. Krailsheimer. Harmondsworth, UK: Penguin, 1966.

Sinkinson, Chris. *Christian Confidence: An Introduction to Defending the Faith*. Downers Grove, IL: InterVarsity Press, 2012.

Sire, James W. *Echoes of a Voice: We Are Not Alone*. Eugene, OR: Cascade Books, 2014.

———. *A Little Primer on Humble Apologetics*. Downers Grove, IL: InterVarsity Press, 2006.

———.*Why Good Arguments Often Fail*. Downers Grove, IL: InterVarsity Press, 2006.

———. *Why Should Anyone Believe Anything at All?* Downers Grove, IL: InterVarsity Press, 1994.

Stackhouse, John. *Humble Apologetics: Defending the Faith Today*. New York: Oxford University Press, 2002.

Templeton, John, and Robert L. Herrmann. *The God Who Would Be Known*. San Francisco: Harper & Row, 1989.

Wiker, Benjamin, and Jonathan Witt. *A Meaningful World: How the Arts and Sciences Reveal the Genius of Nature*. Downers Grove, IL: InterVarsity Press, 2006.

Wright, N. T. *Simply Christian*. San Francisco: HarperSanFrancisco, 2006.

Jesus the Reason

Stott, John R. W. *Basic Christianity.* 2nd ed. Downers Grove, IL: InterVarsity Press, 1970.

Wright, N. T. *Who Is Jesus?* Grand Rapids: Eerdmans, 1992.

Yancey, Philip. *The Jesus I Never Knew.* Grand Rapids: Zondervan, 1995.

The Resurrection of Jesus

Habermas, Gary, and Anthony Flew. *Did Jesus Rise from the Dead?* Edited by Terry L. Miethe. San Francisco: Harper & Row, 1987.

Lewis, C. S. *Miracles: A Preliminary Study.* New York: Macmillan, 1947.

Wright, N. T. *Christian Origins and the Question of God.* Vol. 1, *Jesus and the Victory of God*; vol. 2, *The New Testament and the People of God*; vol. 3, *The Resurrection of the Son of God.* Minneapolis: Fortress, 1996–2003.

The Historical Reliability of the Bible

Barnett, Paul. *Is the New Testament Reliable?* Downers Grove, IL: InterVarsity Press, 1986.

Blomberg, Craig. *The Historical Reliability of the Gospels.* Downers Grove, IL: InterVarsity Press, 1987.

Evans, Craig A. *Fabricating Jesus: How Modern Scholars Distort the Gospels.* Downers Grove, IL: InterVarsity Press, 2006.

Witherington, Ben, III. *The Jesus Quest: The Third Search for the Jew of Nazareth.* 2nd ed. Downers Grove, IL: InterVarsity Press, 1997.

INDEX